To ENDA

GREAT
GAA MOMENTS
2006

by

Finbarr McCarthy

MENTOR
BOOKS

First Published in 2006 by

MENTOR BOOKS
43 Furze Road,
Sandyford Industrial Estate,
Dublin 18,
Republic of Ireland.

Tel: + 353 1 295 2112 / 3   Fax: + 353 1 295 2114
e-mail: admin@mentorbooks.ie
www.mentorbooks.ie

ISBN 10: 1-84210-374-1
ISBN 13: 978-1-84210-374-6

A catalogue record for this book
is available from the British Library

Edited by: Treasa O'Mahony

Design and layout by: Kathryn O'Sullivan

Cover design by: Graham Thew

Photos supplied by: www.sportsfile.com
Ger McCarthy

Printed in Ireland by ColourBooks Ltd.

1 3 5 7 9 10 8 6 4 2

CONTENTS

ACKNOWLEDGEMENTS

When my phone rang one Wednesday morning in February 2006 little did I realise that a few short months later I would have written a book.

I entered this project with a mixture of fear and anxiety, but also stimulated by the challenge and reassured by the support of so many.

Danny McCarthy from Mentor Books was fantastic. His help was always there and his words of wisdom were a constant source of encouragement.

From our first meeting, where he outlined his idea (and it was his idea) over a cup of coffee and a scone in Heuston Station he has displayed unstinting faith in my ability to write this book, more so than myself at times. Danny, I hope the finished project will justify the faith you had in me.

Treasa sent me back a 'marked' copy of my first article. My reaction was 'no way will I do this book'. However, she reassured me that it was normal procedure and not to worry. Since then, Treasa's support and words have helped me no end and I am forever grateful for that.

Kathryn, who was responsible for the design and layout, has done a wonderful job and the finished book is a tribute to her skills.

My thanks too to Shane Coleman of the *Sunday Tribune* for all his help.

Since entering the media game in 1996, as a late developer, I have enjoyed wonderful working relationships with so many people in print, radio and TV. Their help was always forthcoming. Any time I approached someone for information, it was immediately forwarded.

In this regard my thanks to Cian Murphy, Peter Sweeney, Gordon Manning and Karl O'Kane of *The Star* newspaper, Kieran Shannon of the *Sunday Tribune*, Ian O'Riordan of *The Irish Times*, Jim O'Sullivan of the *Irish Examiner*, not forgetting my good friend Michael Clifford, formerly of the *Evening Echo* in Cork now with the *Daily Mail*, Sean Walsh of Galway Bay FM and RTÉ's Marty Morrissey.

My colleagues in 96/103 FM Sport, especially Barry O'Mahoney who gave me my first break, Michael Scanlon, Sean Barry, Ronan McManamay, Kieran O'Driscoll, John Cashman, Paudie Palmer and Jim Nolan, the staff of the *Cork Independent* and also Eddie Lyons who, as editor of the now departed *Inside Cork*, allowed me pen my own weekly column.

Family and friends are very important and without the unstinting support of my wife Mary I doubt if I would have got through the year. Her critical eye over my stories spotted many an error and for that a very special thanks.

My brothers Thomas and Donal were always there when needed, as was my good friend Pat Keane.

My parents in-law Nora and John Joe's lovely bungalow in Crosshaven was the perfect location for hours of peaceful and uninterrupted work – thanks a lot – as was the support of all my relations who gave me huge encouragement.

When approached to write this book the first person I asked for advice was Damian Lawlor of the *Sunday Independent*. It was the shrewdest move I ever made. Damian has been a great friend since his time in Cork, and it is a friendship I value. During the past few months he has been a constant rock, advising, guiding, encouraging and supporting me at all times. Thanks mate.

I have been involved in the GAA for many years now, some would say too many. In that time I have met some fantastic people who have helped me along the way. A special word though for Mary's uncle Dave O'Brien whose worldly advice has steered me in the right direction, thanks Dave.

A special thanks to GAA President Nickey Brennan for writing the *Foreword* and who without hesitation agreed to preside over the launch of the book in Dublin. Best of luck to Nickey in his term as Uachtarán.

Thanks also to John Allen for doing me the honour of launching the book in my native Cork. John is one of nature's gentleman and in the last few years he has been very helpful to me with my work for 96/103 FM Sport. All the best for the future to John.

To Sportsfile (Philip Kinnane and Ray McManus) for permission to use their excellent photographs. Thanks too to Ger McCarthy for his wonderful images.

My thanks also to Anthony Savage of the Rochestown Park Hotel, Catherine Tiernan and Pat Madigan of O2 and again to Ronan and Sean of 96 FM for their generous sponsorship of the book launch.

Thanks also to my club colleagues in St Nick's/ Glen Rovers, especially Jerry Howe, and to the Senior Football team, who have given us such 'great' moments in the last few months.

And last, but most certainly, not least, my heartfelt thanks to the footballers, hurlers and camogie players of the 32 counties. Without them, this book could not exist.

I have really enjoyed writing this book and I sincerely hope that those of you who read it will get as much enjoyment as I did.

Finbarr McCarthy
September 2006

FOREWORD
by
Nickey Brennan
President of the GAA

Is mian liom comhghairdeas a ghabháil le Fionnbarra Mac Cháthraigh as an dea-obair a rinne sé chun an foilsiúchán seo a chur le chéile. Tugann sé deis dúinn ár n-aigne a dhíriú ar laethanta iontacha an t-samhraidh agus beidh seans ag daoine i gcéin is i gcongar taithneamh a bhaint as an ngaiscíocht a léirigh ár n-imreoirí sa bhlian 2006. Is iontach go bhfuil na scéalta go léir curtha i gcló ag Fionnbarra.

It is always a major topic of discussion as to whether the current year's hurling and football championships lived up to the expectations of supporters or whether they were up to the standards of recent years. While two traditionalists, Kerry and Kilkenny, ended the year with the major titles, the 2006 championships served up plenty of enthralling contests. Kerry and Kilkenny may not have been the favourites at the start of the year, but they were seen as very strong contenders. Both were worthy champions.

Kilkenny won another Under 21 Hurling title but Tipperary will feel justifiably frustrated that they did not secure victory in the drawn game. A major highlight of the year was the victory of Mayo in the Under 21 Football Final. Cork looked in a commanding position at half time in that final but Mayo put in a powerful second half to capture a long overdue All-Ireland title. The famine was over at last and the relief and excitement on the faces of both the Mayo players and supporters in Ennis that afternoon was a joy to behold.

The minor grades also threw up plenty of exciting hurling and football, particularly in the two All-Ireland Finals. The high standards were set earlier in the year when the Colleges Finals threw up two absorbing contests in Carlow, with the Dublin Colleges and Abbey CBS from Newry capturing their first titles.

We had a Galway double in the club championships with Portumna

(Hurling) and Salthill Knocknacarra (Football) victorious. Another milestone in 2006 was the playing of the Intermediate and Junior Club finals in Croke Park. The players from the eight participating clubs will always remember their big day at Headquarters.

Camogie's big day was shared with the Under 21 All-Ireland Hurling Final and the experiment will be continued in 2007. Cork scored a very comfortable win over Tipperary in the final and look set for a period of dominance. The Cork ladies' football continues to dominate also and it is remarkable that so many dual players are able and indeed willing to cope with the demands of the two codes.

On a personal level the staging of Féile na nGael in Cork and Féile Peil na nÓg in Wicklow were undoubted highlights. Both Féile competitions bring out the best in every host club where a warm welcome awaits the visitors from around Ireland and overseas. The opportunity to represent your county in Féile is a big thrill for every club. I am already looking forward to next year when the Hurling Féile will be staged in Kilkenny and the Football Féile in Leitrim, Sligo and Roscommon.

I compliment Finbarr McCarthy on this fine publication, which includes some wonderful memories of 2006 in pictures and stories. Finbarr is firstly a club man, but is also a well known commentator on all GAA matters. His immense knowledge of Gaelic Games makes him well qualified to recall the 'Great GAA Moments of 2006'.

The publication will make for a wonderful read as we head into the conclusion of GAA activities for 2006.

Nioclás Ó Braonáin
Uachtarán
Cumann Lúthchleas Gael

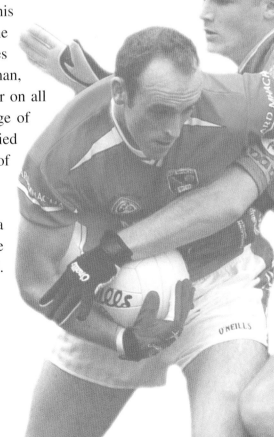

This book is dedicated to
my late parents
Bridgie and Finbarr.
'Keep in touch'

Derek Savage, Galway, tries to retain possession despite the attention of James Nallen, Mayo. Mayo v Galway, National Football League, Division 1 Semi Final, McHale Park, Castlebar, Co. Mayo. 16 April 2006

ALLIANZ NATIONAL FOOTBALL LEAGUE

The opening day of the Allianz National Football League may have been dominated by the 'Omagh Brawl' but as the competition progressed it produced some outstanding and exciting matches.

On the final day of the group games, practically every county had something to play for.

For some it was a semi final spot, while for others it was the desire to avoid the drop to Division 2.

In Division 2, the Waterford footballers, a team not renowned for grabbing the headlines, defeated Cavan in Kingspan Breffni Park.

This rare away win denied Cavan not only promotion to Division B, but also a place in the semi final and an opportunity to generate some badly-needed finance for the county board.

Interestingly in Division 2, Sligo manager Dominic Corrigan was sacked by the county board after just two games. The board was unhappy that the team lost both matches and was effectively out of the race for promotion.

There was an added ingredient in the mix: on the final day of the group games, the Gaelic Players Association in their ongoing dispute with the GAA organised a fifteen-minute delay to the games.

This was adhered to at all venues but some matches started ahead of others. As a result, the fate of a few counties hung in the balance until all games were completed.

Group phase

The real story of Division 1 was in Section A where All Ireland champions Tyrone played their way back into contention following defeats in their opening two games.

Mayo, now under Mickey Moran, were the early pacesetters but a heavy loss to Dublin in the penultimate round left them vulnerable.

Kerry were eyeing a semi final

spot, while Fermanagh and Dublin also harboured similar ambitions but were dependent on results elsewhere.

Two out of the three teams at the bottom of the group (Cork, Monaghan and Offaly), would be relegated to Division 2.

Cork condemned Monaghan to relegation by winning in Castleblayney, their first victory away from home in three years. However, even a big win over Fermanagh could not save Offaly as they departed Division 1.

April 9th was dubbed 'Calculator Sunday' such were the possible permutations that could emerge from the various games.

The key matches were Mayo and Tyrone in Castlebar and the clash of old rivals Kerry and Dublin in Killarney.

Tyrone needed a win to secure a semi final berth while Kerry had to beat Dublin and then hope the Ulster side would drop points to give the Kingdom a place in the last four.

There was a dramatic conclusion to the game in Killarney. A late Conal Keaney point earned Dublin a draw – their first point gained on 'Kerry soil' since 1982. That game finished ahead of the natch in Castlebar and Kerry boss ack O'Connor was resigned to his side losing out.

However, there was another wist to the drama. They were still playing and it was level in Castlebar when Tyrone won a corable free.

The normally reliable Stephen O'Neill took the wrong option, Mayo won possession and with hat the full-time whistle sounded. Tyrone were out, Kerry and Mayo vere in and even the draw in Killarney couldn't save Dublin.

There was plenty to play for as vell in Division 1B with some big guns among those fighting for urvival.

Of the eight teams in the group, our were in contention for the emi finals while the other four vere battling to avoid relegation.

The previous year, 2005, Armagh and unfashionable Wexford contested the League inal. Armagh won their only title o date in Croke Park before a huge crowd. Now they were in Wexford Park and the prize on offer was survival.

Mattie Forde's excellence kept Wexford in the game for long periods. However, the win they craved was denied them when Steven McDonnell of Armagh hit a fabulous late point.

It sent the men from the Model County crashing out of Division 1 and it also preserved Armagh's status in the top flight.

There was even more drama in Páirc Tailteann in Navan as Meath and Derry played out a thriller.

In his first season at the helm, Meath manager Eamonn Barry had endured a traumatic few months. Now his reshaped team were in a battle to stay in Division 1 having just gained promotion after languishing in Division 2 for a few years.

Meath won by a point and were actually celebrating on the field when results from elsewhere filtered through.

Joy quickly turned to despair as reality dawned. Even their first win over Derry in twenty years was not enough for Meath to avoid relegation. It meant a quick return to Division 2. Eamonn Barry's reign was off to the worst possible start.

With Wexford and Meath relegated, attention now switched to the top of the table and here it was just as exciting.

Laois and Down were in pole positions. With Derry's defeat, a chink of light had appeared for Peter Forde's Galway as they faced Down in Newcastle.

The all-Leinster clash of Laois and Kildare petered out in a tame draw. Kildare were guaranteed mid-table survival and Laois were through to the semi final.

Galway went on a goal-scoring burst and with Michael Meehan in sparkling form, it ensured a win for the Connacht side. That and a combination of other results propelled Galway into the semi final and Down were out.

So when the dust had settled, two unlikely semi final pairings emerged. For the first time since 2002, Ulster was not represented in the last four.

It paired Mick O'Dwyer's Laois with his native Kerry in Killarney and an all-Connacht clash of Galway and Mayo in Castlebar with both venues decided on the toss of a coin.

A crowd of over 11,000 turned up in Fitzgerald Stadium, Killarney on Easter Sunday to see if Mick O'Dwyer's Laois could outwit his native county at a venue where he had enjoyed many a good day.

It started brightly enough for the O'Moore county men and they led early on. However, the absence of two key players – Aiden Fennelly and Chris Conway – weakened their challenge.

As the first half wore on, even when playing against the wind, Kerry improved,

Ronan O'Connor, Kerry, in action against Brian McCormack, Laois. Allianz National Football League Division 1 Semi Final, Kerry v Laois, Fitzgerald Stadium, Killarney, Co. Kerry. 16 April 2006 principally because Dara O'Sé and Kieran Donaghy got a grip in midfield.

Defensively, Kerry contained the Laois attack, thus allowing time and space to build attacking movements.

The signs were ominous for Laois – with just twenty minutes played, Kerry were 0-6 to 0-3 ahead and in control in most areas.

Indeed were it not for Laois goalkeeper Fergal Byron, the margin would have been greater as twice in quick succession he denied Colm Cooper certain goals.

However, with the game in first half injury time, the killer blow arrived.

The Laois defence were marked absent and standing in splendid isolation. Cooper on this occasion slipped the ball under Byron's diving body to leave it 1-8 to 0-5 for Kerry at the break.

It meant the second half would be a pretty mundane affair and so it proved as Kerry without really moving up a gear retained the initiative as Laois struggled.

To their credit, they battled away and were denied a goal when former Austin Stack's man Billy

Sheehan's shot came back off the crossbar before being ushered to safety by Kerry. It was that kind of afternoon.

In the end, Kerry were comfortable winners, with manager Jack O'Connor commenting that 'it's good to be in the final as quality matches are better than a month's training'.

Laois boss Mick O'Dwyer was philosophical to the point of saying, 'it didn't really matter. After all, it was 'only' the league!'

Semi Finals
Kerry **1-15**
Laois **0-10**

The all-Connacht clash [Mayo v Galway] never really sparkled. Many in the crowd of 10,768 were heading for the exits in McHale Park, Castlebar long before the finish, the majority of them Mayo supporters.

Games between these two fierce rivals generally produce good football but this contest had more negatives than positives, and the outcome was never really in doubt.

They both entered the game with contrasting form. Mayo, for so long the pacesetters in the group stages, began to ship water with the finishing line in sight.

Galway improved with every outing. Eventually, like a well-trained thoroughbred, they sprinted into the semi final with a strong finishing burst, which they maintained in this game.

Tactically, manager Peter Forde got it right, outsmarting a team he once managed. He thus repeated his trick of the 2005 Connacht final.

In many respects, it mirrored the game in Killarney. Done and dusted by the three-quarter mark, Galway were in control, leading by 1-9 to 0-5 with Matthew Clancy's 29th minute goal proving crucial.

Padraig Joyce and Michael Donnellan played important roles. Not even the introduction of the enigmatic Ciarán McDonald could save Mayo.

Austin O'Malley did get a Mayo goal in the 58th minute but despite the backing of a strong wind, they could add only one more point. And once again their old failing of underperforming on the big day surfaced as they exited a competition they had dominated for so long.

Galway **1-11**
Mayo **1-6**

The Gaelic Grounds in Limerick, with the Cratloe Hills in the background, was the venue for the decider. However, the timing of the match caused uproar, especially in Kerry.

Five-thirty on a Sunday afternoon was not only 'unacceptable, but downgrading the competition as is the decision to move the game from Croke Park' according to an angry Sean Walsh, Chairman of the Kerry County Board.

There were mitigating factors, not least the Munster v Leinster Heineken Cup rugby semi final in Lansdowne Road.

As a consequence of this, a paltry attendance of 7,598 witnessed a contest that never really dazzled.

Galway started brightly and with their highly-rated attack looking dangerous, they had plenty of possession. However, a failure to translate it into scores proved costly.

The Connacht men bossed that opening half and their policy of a crowded defence left Kerry danger man Colm 'Gooch' Cooper completely isolated.

In fact, Galway corner-back Damien Burke did an exceptional job on Cooper in that half, but it was a different story in the second period.

Galway led at half-time by 0-6 to 0-3. It was not a reflection of their dominance, as Kerry went twenty-six minutes without a score in the half.

Wing back Mossie Lyons' point in the 34th minute was only Kerry's second from play. Cooper pointed a free and full-forward Declan O'Sullivan also scored.

As the sides trooped off at the break, Kerry selectors Jack O'Connor, Ger O'Keeffe and Johnny Cullotty stood on the sideline, calmly discussing their options. What they came up with changed the direction of the game.

Just before the break, the ineffective Ronan O'Connor was called ashore, while Eamonn Fitzmaurice did not re-appear for the second half.

Eoin Brosnan came on at centre-forward and with Darren O'Sullivan offering more width in attack, Kerry prospered.

Dara O'Sé thundered into the game in midfield, Seamus Moynihan was dominant at centre-back, while Brosnan on the '40' punched holes in the Galway defence.

Kerry scored a few early points, but Galway still led 0-7 to 0-6. Then the game's first goal arrived in the 53rd minute. It proved the pivotal score.

Cooper created it with a lovely pass to Paul Galvin and the Finuge man drilled the ball into the net, passed a helpless Alan Keane.

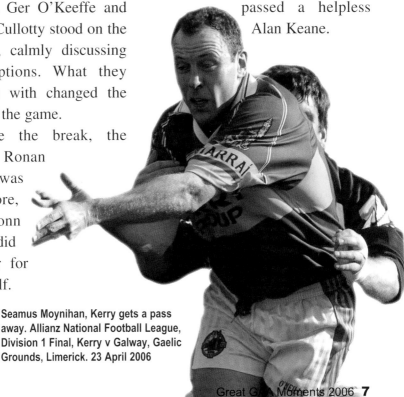

Seamus Moynihan, Kerry gets a pass away. Allianz National Football League, Division 1 Final, Kerry v Galway, Gaelic Grounds, Limerick. 23 April 2006

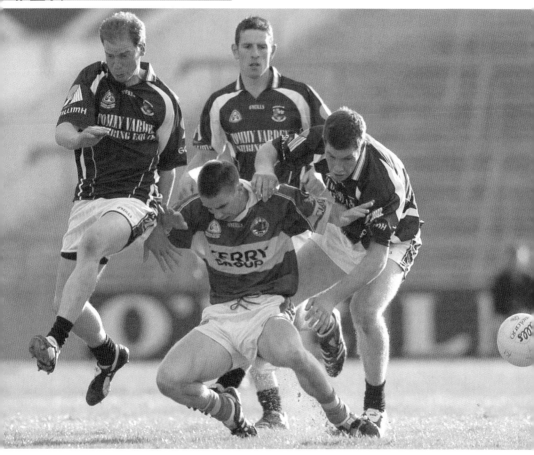

Marc O'Sé, Kerry, is tackled by Galway players – from left Michael Donnellan, Alan Burke and Niall Coleman. Allianz National Football League, Division 1 Final, Kerry v Galway, Gaelic Grounds, Limerick. 23 April 2006

Galway were now struggling – the much vaunted attack starved of possession saw Sean Armstrong replaced. Padraig Joyce added just one point from play, while Michael Meehan failed to raise a flag of any colour in the second half.

Kerry's second goal arrived in the 61st minute and it was created and finished by the Dr Croke's club duo of Cooper and Brosnan. Cooper was again the creator, while Brosnan's finish was top class. Game over.

In the end, it resembled a stroll in the evening sun as Kerry eased to a comfortable victory. This was their second title in three years and their third successive league final victory over Galway (1984 and 2004 were the others). It was also their 18th National League Football title.

Galway will regret their first half failings in the scoring stakes, while Kerry boss Jack O'Connor was delighted at winning: 'It was a very good second-half display and we can now look forward to the championship.'

It was O'Connor's fifth title with Kerry in his three years as manager.

A special day too for new GAA President Nickey Brennan as he performed his first official duty by presenting the Allianz National Football league cup to Kerry captain, Dromid-Pearses man, Declan O'Sullivan.

It was a pity though that a competition which began with a bang (remember the 'Omagh Brawl'?) should end so tamely as it produced exciting fare along the way.

The crowd was the smallest in memory for a league final, even falling below the paltry 9,000 who attended the Cork v Dublin final in 1999, a game also played at an unusual time of 2pm in Páirc Uí Chaoimh. By comparison, 46,000 witnessed the 2005 final between Wexford and Armagh, while in February 2006 over 20,000 watched Tyrone and Armagh in the McKenna Cup semi final.

On the same afternoon in Kingspan Breffni Park, Cavan, over 12,000 watched Donegal and Louth play out a thrilling draw in the Division 2 final. Louth won the replay.

The size of the crowd will not trouble Kerry as they headed home on a sunny April evening with yet another piece of silverware safely tucked under their arms, and with an eye on an even bigger prize as the season unfolds.

Final
Kerry **2-12**
Galway **0-10**

Tyrone manager Mickey Harte and Dublin manager Paul Caffrey share a few words after the final whistle. Tyrone v Dublin, Healy Park, Omagh, Co. Tyrone. 5 February 2006

OMAGH BRAWL
Sunday February 5th, 2006

All Ireland champions 2005 Tyrone met Leinster champions Dublin in a match that made headlines for weeks afterwards . . . but not for the football.

The match: It was the perfect match with which to open the Allianz National Football League. A clash between the All Ireland champions Tyrone and Leinster champions Dublin. Dublin's loyal and colourful band of supporters would guarantee a big crowd in Healy Park, Omagh and with the TG4 cameras present, the stay-at-home supporter would also enjoy the best of the action. Remember these two teams met twice in the Championship back in August 2005 and produced two thrillers, but this would be oh so different!

There was a strange atmosphere surrounding the ground that February afternoon.

Maybe it was the fact that the 'Dubs' did not give Tyrone the traditional guard of honour afforded the All Ireland champions on their first league outing of the season. Afterwards, when this 'oversight' was put to the Dublin management, a spokesperson said 'Tyrone were out on the field early and did not return to the dressing room before the throw in'.

Experienced referee Paddy Russell got proceedings underway and within four minutes he produced the first of what amounted to a total of eighteen yellow cards when he booked Alan Brogan (Dublin) and Brian Meenan (Tyrone). It set the trend for a fractious afternoon.

The bookings steadily continued and by thirty minutes into the game, it was evident that as a spectacle this was slowly turning into an ugly contest. The paying customer, in excess of 6,000 of them, was witnessing something that had little resemblance to a football match.

In fact, in a blunt after-match comment Tyrone manager Mickey Harte said 'no supporter should have to watch such behaviour and it did little for the image of Gaelic Football . . . I felt sorry for those people who came today hoping to see a good game of football. It was anything but.' This was the only attempt at an apology from either team management in the aftermath of the game.

The most serious of all the incidents occurred within sixty seconds of the start of the second half. Alan Brogan received a second yellow card for a clash with Ciaran Gourley and was dismissed. On leaving the field, Brogan exchanged words with Tyrone's Medical Officer, Dr Seamus Cassidy. Ciaran Whelan then got involved, thus initiating another row in which several players from both sides joined in.

A Tyrone player, Michael McGee, grabbed Brogan and immediately a mass brawl broke out. Over thirty players were involved and it spilled quickly over to the sideline. The frightened look on the faces of the supporters, young and old, male and female in the stand quite close to the incident, told its own story.

When order had been restored, Colin Holmes from Tyrone was sent off. Amazingly, he was the only player to be disciplined from this incident, the one that grabbed the major share of the headlines.

The game continued, as did the niggling from both sets of players. Eventually, two more players were sent off. Along with the 18 yellow cards, Paddy Russell also issued 4 red cards, 2 to each side. When it was all over – incidental though it may seem – Dublin won the match 1-9 to 1-6, but that result was overshadowed in the days that followed as the fallout continued and the investigations began. The drama was far from over.

Condemnation

The condemnation when it arrived was swift and to the point. GAA President Sean Kelly said 'such scenes have no place in our association as it sends out all the wrong signals, especially when two of our top teams that contain many household names are involved in such disgraceful incidents. The matter will be fully and quickly investigated and those who have been found to be in breach of the rules will be dealt with accordingly.'

Sympathy was expressed for referee Paddy Russell who many felt should have abandoned the game. Others took the view that this course of action could have led to even more trouble and he did very well to ensure the match was brought to its conclusion.

Interestingly, well-respected journalist and former Offaly manager Eugene McGee speaking on Setanta Sports' programme *The Hub* the following Monday said, 'what was very disturbing was that neither the Dublin nor Tyrone County Boards issued an apology to the fans and the GAA in general after what were the most appalling scenes we witnessed at a major game in a long numbers of years, preferring to trot out the time honoured reply, 'we await a copy of the referee's report before we comment,' which in this instance is just not good enough'.

It is said that a picture paints a thousand words and the graphic images of the scenes in Monday's and subsequent days' newspapers did little for the footballing reputations of the counties and indeed the GAA as a whole.

The incident dominated the

Tyrone and Dublin players involved in a mass brawl on the sideline during the second half.
Tyrone v Dublin, Healy Park, Omagh, Co. Tyrone. 5 February 2006

airwaves nationally and locally for a few days, but if the GAA thought the matter would be swiftly brought to a satisfactory conclusion, then they got it badly wrong, as the fallout continued for quite some time.

The Investigation and its Findings

The incident set the newly formed Central Disciplinary Committee of the GAA and Chairman Con Hogan (Tipperary) yet another severe test. Having had some of its most important decisions overturned on appeal in the eleven months since its formation, the view within the GAA was simply they had to get this one right.

So after the drama on the field, focus now switched to the 'committee' who were about to sit and judge those players whose behaviour had left a sour taste.

Within three days the referee's report was with the CDC. Despite earlier indications, the committee resisted the temptation to issue immediate sanctions and instead charged seven players and one official with various offences.

Colin Holmes (Tyrone) was automatically suspended for four weeks having received a straight red card, while his colleagues Michael McGee, Owen Mulligan and Kevin Hughes were charged under Rule 140 (discrediting the association), with the latter two also being charged under Rule 138.

Dublin's Ciaran Whelan, Kevin Bonner and Alan Brogan were all charged under Rule 140, with Brian Cullen being charged under Rule 138. Both the Tyrone and Dublin County Boards were also charged with bringing the association into disrepute, while Tyrone's Dr Seamus Cassidy was summoned to appear before the CDC, a committee now firmly under the spotlight as its findings would have major ramifications for both counties.

All the players sought and were granted personal hearings and the committee met twice within the space of seven days before releasing their findings on Sunday February 19th, which was the opening day of the Allianz National Hurling League.

To their credit, the CDC came down hard on players and county boards alike, both of whom were fined €10,000 each. Tyrone's Dr

Seamus Cassidy and Dublin's Peadar Andrews were warned as to their future conduct, while Tyrone defender Ryan McMenamin was cleared of any wrongdoing.

Not so lucky were Dublin's Brogan, Whelan and Bonner [although that would change quickly]. All three received eight weeks suspension as did Tyrone's McGee, Mulligan and Hughes. The latter two were also given a further four weeks but it was to run concurrently. One other player, Dublin's Brian Cullen, received a four week suspension which allowed him to play with DCU in the Sigerson Cup in which they were acting as hosts.

The general opinion was that the findings were fair. GAA President Sean Kelly hoped that 'a line could be drawn in the sand' and those involved would accept their punishment so the Association could move on to doing what it does best:

'Playing our games in the spirit that they were intended to be played in.' His appeal, unlike those of the players, was to fall on deaf ears.

Appeals

The Dublin and Tyrone County Boards decided not to appeal against the fines imposed. However, to the disappointment of many, all the suspended players exercised their democratic right under GAA rules to appeal, ensuring the 'Omagh Incident' rumbled on.

All the suspended players lodged appeals with the Central Appeals Committee (CAC) and although it was the players who appealed, they did so with the full weight of their respective county boards behind them.

The appeals were quickly heard and the players said afterwards 'they received a very fair hearing and would now await the findings'. However, Tyrone manager Mickey Harte went slightly further and said, 'I feel very confident that the appeals would be successful'. His confidence was well founded.

Within a few days of hearing the appeals, the CAC announced, to the dismay of many and the delight of others, that all seven players had been successful in their appeals and therefore cleared to play with their counties in the

Dublin and Tyrone players scuffle during the game. 5 February 2006

A mass brawl broke out with over thirty players involved and it spilled quickly over to the sideline. Tyrone v Dublin

matches scheduled for the weekend of March 10th/11th.

In an ironic twist, because the football league had a two-week break and the suspensions were lifted, the seven players missed no league game despite their involvement in some of the most disgraceful scenes witnessed on a GAA field in a long number of years.

The appeals were successful on the following technicalities:

(1) The players, as is their right, were not called in by the CDC to review the tape and explain their actions before they were charged.

(2) Three members of the CDC formed a subcommittee which reviewed the tape and then charged the various players. The same three men subsequently sat on the disciplinary hearing, contrary to GAA rules.

Reaction

It is ironic that on the very day that the success of the appeals became public knowledge, the GAA hosted a reception for their inter-county referees in Croke Park. This function also honoured some of the outstanding officials who had retired, and the general feeling among those in attendance was of 'being left down by officialdom' again.

Pat McEnaney and Dickie Murphy, two men who had handled All Ireland Finals, went on record to express their disappointment at the outcome, while at the same time acknowledging the right of the players to appeal. They both had enormous respect for referee Paddy Russell who dealt bravely with a difficult situation and deserved the full support of the authorities. This decision meant that out of a brawl that had brought shame on the counties involved and the GAA, only one player (Tyrone's Colin Holmes) served a meaningful suspension. Referees and officials the length and breadth of the country were asking themselves 'why bother?'

Endgame

So the curtain finally came down on a saga that the opening day of the 2006 Allianz National Football League will always be associated with – the 'Omagh Brawl'. In a match in which there were more cards than scores (eighteen as against seventeen), it is only right to finish with a quote from Dublin manager Paul Caffrey who when asked for his comments immediately after the game, replied, 'well we won and it's two points in the bag'.

A young Galway supporter makes his way to his seat before the game. Tipperary v Galway, Allianz National Hurling League, Division 1B, Round 4, Semple Stadium, Thurles, Co. Tipperary. 26 March 2006

NATIONAL
Hurling League

Babs Keating's quote that his Tipperary players were 'dead only to wash them' may go down as the GAA quote of 2006. However, his players managed to revive themselves – Lazarus like – before the end of the League

By comparison with the football league, the Allianz National Hurling League failed to generate any great enthusiasm, a fact reflected in the meagre attendances at some games.

Kilkenny versus Tipperary is one such example – these two teams always promise an attractive fixture yet this was played in an almost deserted Semple Stadium.

Of course the problem lies in the fact that the number of high quality teams is limited to eight at most. And with several counties adopting a low-key approach to the league, it is easy to see where the apathy came from.

Different teams had different needs from the league. Cork, for instance, made no secret of the fact that they would use it to try out players in advance of the Championship.

Tipperary, with Babs Keating back in charge, were keen to make an impression and before the competition had ran its course, Babs was in the news again.

After a traumatic few years during which they had as many managers as matches, Limerick presented a united front and were determined to lay down a marker. Offaly were bidding to recapture lost pride after a mauling from Kilkenny in the 2005 Championship.

What was evident from early on was that Down and Laois were clearly out of their depth in this company and were destined for the relegation series.

Down, to their credit and despite the resignation of their manager midway through the campaign, survived by defeating Laois in the play-off final.

A huge boost for the hurling folk in the beautiful Ards Peninsula.

Antrim started brightly by winning their opening two games, including a great win over Galway.

However, their optimism was short-lived and along with Wexford, they were sucked into the battle to stay in Division 1. Both survived.

The best performance of the group stages came from Kilkenny who hammered fierce rivals Tipperary. Were it not for the heroics of goalkeeper Brendan Cummins, it would have been a humiliation for Tipperary.

In fact, there was even more excitement after the game, when Tipperary boss Babs Keating let rip at his players over their approach to the game.

Babs – forthright as ever – said many things; but it was his comment that the Tipperary players were 'dead only to wash them' that will go down as the quote of the year. Those comments clearly took from what was an outstanding performance by Kilkenny. The 'Cats' were to do it again before the league ran its course.

It was somewhat ironic that in the final round of the competition, Kilkenny's victory in Galway not only knocked Galway out but also helped secure a quarter final spot for Tipperary. There was life in the bodies yet, or was there?

Meanwhile, Limerick under Joe McKenna were working away quietly. An unbeaten run, including a draw with Kilkenny, saw them qualify for the quarter final from Division 1B.

In Division 1A, Clare, Offaly, Waterford and Cork were all in contention entering the penultimate round. However, the cancellation of the Cork v Wexford game caused a problem.

In an effort to ensure no county had an advantage, the final round of games was deferred for a week as the Cork v Wexford game was re-fixed.

Cork's easy win consigned Wexford to the relegation dogfight and set up an intriguing last day. For once, the crowds came out.

Offaly had enjoyed a good campaign but still needed to beat Waterford in Birr to prolong their interest in the competition. Waterford were also conscious of the importance of getting something from the game; unfortunately all they got was a host of problems.

Offaly won with a bit to spare, but the real talking point was the dismissal of Waterford's Eoin Kelly for a rash pull. His suspension ruled him out of several important games.

Crucially though, Waterford were still in the competition, simply because of events in Páirc Uí Rinn where almost 7,000 spectators watched as Cork and Clare played out a thriller with Championship fervour.

With ten minutes to go, Cork were in front and looking at a semi final place. Five minutes remaining, it was level. Due to events in Birr, both were in the quarter finals.

However, two late points gave Clare victory and a semi final berth. Cork got their marching orders and the 'Decie's' were thrown a lifeline and the last qualifying place on offer.

So an uneventful group phase ground to its

conclusion and Kilkenny and Clare went directly into the semi finals.

Tipperary were set to play Offaly in one quarter final and Limerick were due to play Waterford in the other. A double header in Thurles would be the first big occasion of the hurling year.

QUARTER FINALS
Tipperary v Offaly

Of the two sides in this clash, Offaly had less to lose, if you could use such a phrase about the quarter final of a national competition.

This match would tell manager John McIntyre exactly how far his reshaped Offaly team had progressed over the spring and if they had the capacity to make an impact in the Championship.

As it transpired, he learned a lot, even in defeat. His young and energetic side gave their more fancied opponents a testing seventy minutes. At the end, the manager was quick to say 'no complaints, we gave it our best shot and we will be a better team as a result'.

Tipperary won a quality contest simply because they finished stronger. It was level at 2-15 to 3-12 after 55 minutes. However, in the closing quarter, six points eased the home side through to a rematch with Kilkenny and an opportunity for the 'bodies' to rise and redeem themselves.

Tipperary	**.... 2-21**
Offaly	**....... 3-14**

Waterford v Limerick

Waterford entered this game on the back of a very poor display in Birr a week earlier. They exited the game and the competition with yet another major worry to contend with as the Championship approached.

Not only they did lose by seven points, they also lost

Hugh Moloney, Tipperary, makes a diving attempt to stop Eoin Larkin, Kilkenny. Kilkenny v Tipperary.
23 April 2006

their shape and discipline as team captain Paul Flynn was sent off with a straight red-card at a time when the match as a contest was over.

Very few Waterford players emerged from the game with any degree of credit – Ken McGrath, John Mullane and Tony Browne were the exception.

Limerick by contrast were in buoyant mood, as they maintained their unbeaten run and set up a semi final meeting with neighbours Clare.

Manager Joe McKenna was in upbeat form, 'there was much to admire about our hurling in the last twenty minutes, we're starting to motor and you cannot but benefit from games of this nature'.

Limerick led at half-time by 0-8 to 0-7 having played with the wind and the lead did not look enough.

McKenna, however, reshaped his team for the second half. Stephen Lucey came on and he moved Donie Ryan to full-forward. These changes had the desired effect.

Mullane gave Waterford the lead on 50 minutes, but there was no stopping Limerick and when Ryan landed the equaliser on 52 minutes, the die was cast for Justin McCarthy's men.

Limerick were in total control and scored some fabulous points to close out the game. The final rub for Waterford came with the dismissal of their captain. It crowned a day they would quickly want to forget.

Limerick **0-21**
Waterford **0-14**

SEMI FINALS
Limerick v Clare

For long periods of this game, Clare were in control but Joe McKenna along with Ger Cunningham revived the fortunes of Limerick, and they played with a new-found spirit.

Limerick got two first-half goals and rangy full-forward Brian Begley was an instrumental figure in both.

Brian Lohan hauled him down in the second minute and Mark Keane blasted the resultant penalty into the net. In the twelfth minute, Begley himself lashed in goal number two.

Clare, however, were hurling well. Their first goal had a touch of good fortune about it, but it helped them to an interval lead of 1-10 to 2-4.

The gap was down to the bare minimum by the 45th minute, when Niall Gilligan got Clare's second goal. It signalled a good period for Anthony Daly's side.

Thirteen minutes from time, Clare's lead was a commanding 2-17 to 2-8, and Limerick's 15-match unbeaten run looked like it was at an end.

However, displaying all the characteristics that epitomised McKenna's own playing career, Limerick fought back.

A succession of points followed, and with their supporters in the small crowd of just under 10,000 (a certain Munster rugby match in Dublin was a counter attraction) urging them on, they cut the lead to a single point, as the game headed for injury time.

Twice in the closing stages, Clare goalkeeper Davy Fitzgerald pulled off brilliant saves to deny Limerick goals. One such stop was at the expense of a '65', which Mark Keane pointed to send the game into extra-time.

The momentum was now with Limerick. Memories of Clare's fade-out to Cork in the 2005 All Ireland semi final came flooding back, as they wilted in the heat that enveloped Semple Stadium, Thurles.

There was only one team in it in the extra-time. In fact, Clare only got one point in the second period. Limerick took control and with some excellent points eased to victory and a place in the league final.

Limerick	3-23
Clare	2-23

(after extra-time)

Tipperary v Kilkenny

This was billed as the main game of the afternoon, but it fell way short of that. In truth it turned out to be one long yawn, and for Tipperary another trimming at the hands of their great rivals.

A few weeks earlier, the sides met in a group game and Kilkenny won in a canter. Surely pride alone would dictate that this time Tipperary would at least compete.

In fact the opposite happened and by the eleventh minute Kilkenny had plundered two goals, courtesy of James 'Cha' Fitzpatrick and Martin Comerford.

The home side was in disarray and at one stage the scoreboard made for embarrassing reading –

Kilkenny 2-11 Tipperary 0-2 – and not yet half-time.

A goal from Eoin Kelly and a couple of points put some degree of respectability on it as the sides trooped off at half-time, but by now the only thing to be decided was the winning margin.

The second half was a mundane affair. Tipperary improved, but Kilkenny, content the job was done, were only going through the motions.

In the end, twelve points divided the teams, but the gulf in class was much more as Kilkenny headed for their fourth final in six years. Tipperary and Babs retreated to the safety of the dressing room. This time the manager held his counsel. After all the scoreboard told its own story.

Kilkenny 3-20
Tipperary 2-11

FINAL
Kilkenny v Limerick
In keeping with the trend of earlier games, a small crowd of 16,500 attended the final on a day when drizzling rain spat from the skies and a blanket of cloud covered the 'Devil's Bit' mountain behind Ardan Uí Riann in Semple Stadium, Thurles.

It was the fourth meeting of the counties in a league final. Limerick's last win came in 1997, while Kilkenny were seeking to retain their title, a feat they last achieved in 1983 with a team that included newly-elected GAA President Nickey Brennan. Limerick had been the opposition on that day as well.

Limerick were dealt a blow before a ball was struck when leading marksman Mark Keane was ruled out with a hand injury. Kilkenny were that bit sharper, especially in attack. Not for the first time, their ability to snatch goals at vital times proved the difference between victory and defeat.

As expected from a team on a 16-match unbeaten run, Limerick started well and led by 0-3 to 0-2. They were helped not only by good play from several players, but also by Kilkenny's profligacy in front of goal – they hit eight wides in the first half.

Crucially, the first goal arrived in the twelfth minute. Eoin Larkin was the scorer after a pinpoint pass from Henry Shefflin. Kilkenny were also grateful to goalkeeper James McGarry who

Barry Foley, Limerick, solos past John Tennyson, Kilkenny. National Hurling League, Final. Kilkenny v Limerick, Semple Stadium, Thurles, Co. Tipperary. 30 April 2006

denied Limerick's Andrew O'Shaughnessy and Barry Foley attempts on goal with two brilliant saves.

Approaching half-time Limerick were level at 1-4 to 0-7, but were undone by sloppy defending in added time.

Larkin on this occasion turned provider and it was Shefflin who profited by scoring the second goal. As a result they retired at the break in front by 2-4 to 0-7. It was a significant score.

Limerick exerted strong pressure on the resumption, but for all their hard work they were unable to reduce the deficit. In fact after ten minutes both sides had scored two points. The challengers needed a better return.

Kilkenny were coping well with

Limerick's effort, in particular Tommy Walsh, John Tennyson and effective substitute Willie O'Dwyer.

In attack, James 'Cha' Fitzpatrick and Larkin were also prominent, but ultimately it was Shefflin who struck the decisive goal.

With fourteen minutes remaining, Kilkenny had a three point lead, when goal number three arrived. Again Larkin played a pivotal role when his run unhinged the Limerick defence and Shefflin batted the ball to the net, doubling Kilkenny's lead.

Thereafter, the outcome was never really in doubt, although Limerick were annoyed at the score as they felt in the build-up to the goal, Larkin had deliberately dropped his hurley. Their protestations fell on deaf ears.

In the end, Kilkenny's margin of victory was six points – a true reflection on a game that was well contested in difficult conditions. It was also Brian Cody's 13th time leading Kilkenny to a major title as manager, co-incidentally on a day when they won their 13th league title.

Kilkenny **3-11**
Limerick **0-14**

Afterwards he expressed delight a winning: 'we always take the league seriously, we set out to win it, and having done that we are delighted, the players are delighted with their medals and now and only now will we concentrate on the Championship'.

Limerick manager Jo McKenna, while annoyed at some of referee Diarmuid Kirwan' decisions, especially the awarding of the third goal, conceded that the better team won.

'Naturally we are disappointe at not winning, but we played ver well for long periods, and that i pleasing. We have had a goo campaign and we can now fac the Championship with renewe confidence.'

So one week after assumin office, GAA President Nicke Brennan had the pleasure of presenting the cup to a fellow Kilkenny man – team captai Jackie Tyrell – thus bringing th curtain down on a leagu campaign that never really caugh the imagination of supporters.

Interestingly, speaking in a radi interview Brennan suggested th competition needed a revamp a he felt the best teams should b grouped together to generate mor

Eoin Larkin, Kilkenny, celebrates at the end of the game. Kilkenny v Limerick, National Hurling League Final. Semple Stadium, Thurles, Co. Tipperary. 30 April 2006

interest in what is after all the second biggest national competition. It is a sentiment shared by many.

Finally, on a day when Kilkenny were adding to their ever-growing list of honours, the Dublin hurlers returned to the big time by winning the Division 2 title, defeating Kerry in a dour final by 0-17 to 1-6. And with Dublin Colleges winning the All Ireland Colleges title twenty-four hours later, a revival of the ancient game seemed to be taking place in the capital.

Mention should also be made of the feat of the Mayo hurlers. They put up a brave display in the Division 2 semi final, losing to Kerry by a single point 2-17 to 2-16. Mayo were without their best player Keith Higgins who was on under-21 football duty the same day.

But some things never change: 2006 Allianz National Hurling League Champions – Kilkenny.

Clare manager Ger Loughnane, right, and physio Colm Flynn celebrate Clare's victory after the final whistle. Munster Senior Hurling Chamionship Semi Final Replay, Pairc Ui Chaoimh. 12 June 1999

CLARE AND GER LOUGHNANE CONTROVERSY

A telephone conversation started a sequence of events that sent shock waves through the hurling fraternity in Clare.

It all started with a phone call on December 9, 2005. That Friday, Father Harry Bohan, the Clare hurling selector, and Ger Hartmann, the world renowned injury specialist, had a conversation which would set in train a sequence of events that sent shock waves through the hurling fraternity in Clare. Even who phoned who that day has been disputed. Everything in this saga has.

What is accepted is that in the phone call Father Harry stated his firm belief that Clare were close to winning an All Ireland title, based on their narrow defeat to Cork in the 2005 semi final.

To Bohan's surprise, Hartmann disagreed, claiming Clare's standards of preparation were well short of the top teams.

Hartmann had treated the team's players for the previous ten years at a special rate because of his friendship with the team's physical therapist Colum Flynn. He then offered, in confidence, some recommendations and observations that would benefit the team, based on his own expertise and conversations with Flynn and the Clare players while they were on his treatment table.

Hartmann questioned the core strength and general fitness preparation of some of the players. He also disapproved of manager Anthony Daly publicly admitting in newspaper interviews that he had indulged in a two-day drinking spree after losing to Waterford in the 2004 Championship.

The following Tuesday in Ennis, Hartmann met up with his close friend Flynn. Hartmann had detected from the conversation with Father Harry that Flynn was now a peripheral figure in the Clare set-up. Flynn agreed. It had been that way for about a year.

It was why he was offering his resignation to Pat Fitzgerald, the Clare county secretary. Within three days Hartmann also submitted a letter to Fitzgerald, withdrawing his services to the Clare county board until the circumstances behind Flynn's resignation were investigated.

Flynn had given over thirty years of service to the senior county team. He was their physical trainer when they reached the Munster final in '67, their trainer when they won the League in '77 and their physio when they won the All Ireland in '97. Yet after all that time, the only contact he had with either the team or the board in the two months after his resignation was with Pat Fitzgerald and team goalkeeper Davy Fitzgerald, the father of his granddaughter.

In fact, it was only a month later in January 2006 that the rest of the panel became aware that Flynn and Hartmann were finished with the team.

Flynn was further shocked and

saddened by a letter from the team management on January 25. Hartmann, who received a copy of the letter, was equally irked. In the letter, the team management expressed regret at Flynn's resignation but then implied that Hartmann had informed the selectors through his conversation with Father Harry, that he felt that they (the selectors) were running a seriously unprofessional set-up.

What became clear from the contents of the letter was that comments made by Hartmann in strict confidence to Father Harry were now been attributed to Flynn. The letter concluded, that 'the selectors had the full support of the panel of players and that we are deeply hurt and shocked at these allegations about our character and integrity, and would like to meet you and Ger Hartmann to discuss this situation as soon as possible'.

Hartmann, who received the letter before Flynn, immediately phoned Bohan and lambasted him.

Meanwhile, another scandal was brewing within the Clare hurling community. Details of an award scheme organised by the Clare county board and the *Clare Champion* newspaper emerged.

Ger Loughnane, surprisingly, had been omitted from the best Clare team of the past 25 years.

That prompted *The Irish Times* journalist Ian O'Riordan to ring Hartmann, an old friend from the athletics circuit.

When O'Riordan asked 'Ger what's going on down there in Clare?' he was only aware of Loughnane's omission from the awards. Hartmann knew nothing of the awards; he didn't know what was 'going on' because he was no longer involved with Clare. 'You're no longer involved with Clare?!' O'Riordan said 'Well, that's news to me!'

When O'Riordan pressed Hartmann for the story, Hartmann said he would only oblige if everyone in the saga was contacted. Hartmann informed Flynn and Ger Loughnane to expect a call from O'Riordan.

There were further phone calls over the ensuing days that only added to the controversy. A few hours after O'Riordan's call to Hartmann, Father Harry Bohan was presented with a special merit award at a function in the Armada Hotel in Spanish Point.

For Loughnane, it was too much to bear. First there had been the board's treatment of Flynn, then his own omission and non-invitation to the honours' function and now Bohan's recognition at the same function. Loughnane duly phoned the county chairman Michael McDonagh and to quote the man himself, 'gave him a piece of my mind'.

Loughnane's mobile then started ringing with an incoming call from Flynn. Inadvertently, Loughnane failed to replace his landline phone properly.

McDonagh overheard the entire conversation between Loughnane and Flynn. He was shocked by it.

Loughnane admits that when Flynn asked him what he had done for the weekend, he replied, 'I went out hunting with a gun I borrowed from a friend of mine and put an oil can on top of a barrel'. He then imagined someone's head on the top of the barrel and said 'I hit him every time!'

While Loughnane claims to

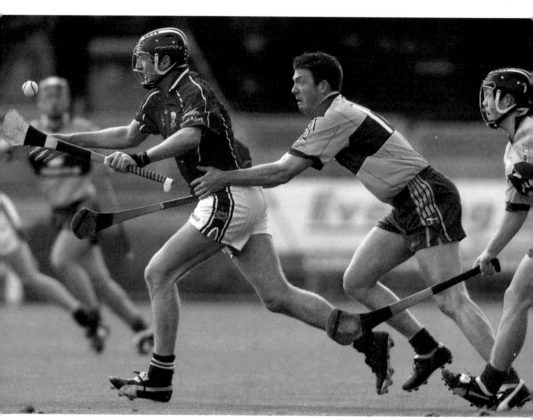

Pat Mulcahy, Cork, tries to get clear of Diarmuid McMahon, Clare. Cork v Clare, Allianz National Hurling League, Páirc Uí Rinn, Cork. 9 April 2006

have been laughing while he was making these comments, he wasn't laughing shortly after he made them. When he finished the call, he heard someone on the speaker phone of his landline.

Then he realised McDonagh had been on the line all along.

McDonagh is a garda detective and based on Loughnane's shotgun-barrel remarks, he made an official complaint to the Gardaí. Loughnane would later try to make light of the conversation but he couldn't laugh off other aspects of the case. In his column in *The Star* newspaper, he criticised the county's team management and county executive for their treatment of Flynn and Hartmann.

Then, in an extraordinary 45-minute interview on Clare FM radio, he described old teammates with whom he won National League medals in 1977 and 1978, as 'big-game chokers'.

He also implicitly criticised Father Harry, the manager of that team, for failing to win the Munster title with that side, even though, just like in his public account of the shotgun-barrel incident, he stopped short of using his name.

Efforts were also made to get McDonagh on the same programme but the county chairman did not wish to comment further. Anthony Daly did go on but not with Loughnane. Daly called for unity in the interest of Clare hurling and appealed for the matter to be, in his words, 'put to bed' so he could get on with preparing his team.

That same weekend, Seanie McMahon, the Clare captain stated that Daly and his management team had the full support of the players. On the Sunday, Clare destroyed Down in the opening game of the league before an appreciative crowd in Ennis.

It was a strange few days. At one point in the 'he said – he said' saga, Daly and Hartmann engaged in text tennis for an hour and a half without coming to an resolution. Indeed, Hartman maintained he would not talk with the management team unless his solicitor was present, such was the breakdown of his relationship with Father Harry.

But then, matters in Clare hurling have obviously been bizarre for years. Father Harry and Loughnane weren't just both key men in the team of '77 and '78 that brought such honour to the county; they're also both from the same small parish of Feakle.

Some things were patched up. Loughnane and McDonagh had a meeting after which the threat of any legal action was withdrawn. Flynn, who Hartmann rightly contends was the real victim in the whole saga, got quickly back to being involved in hurling, helping out his home club, Éire Óg in Ennis.

In his weekly column, Loughnane wished the county team and management well for the coming season. The players got back to doing what they do best – playing hurling. Seemingly unaffected

by what went on, they reached the league semi final.

They seemed to be in control against Limerick, but as they entered the closing stages, they let a good lead slip and were eventually beaten in extra-time.

Then in their rematch with Cork in the first round of the championship, they were soundly beaten. The winning margin was six points but in reality the gap was much wider.

It takes us back then to the comment in the conversation that sparked off this whole GUBU saga, Father Harry's contention that *'We're not far off Cork'*. It prompts the question:

Was Hartmann right after all?

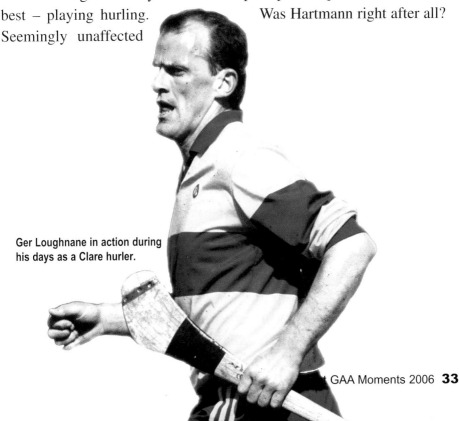

Ger Loughnane in action during his days as a Clare hurler.

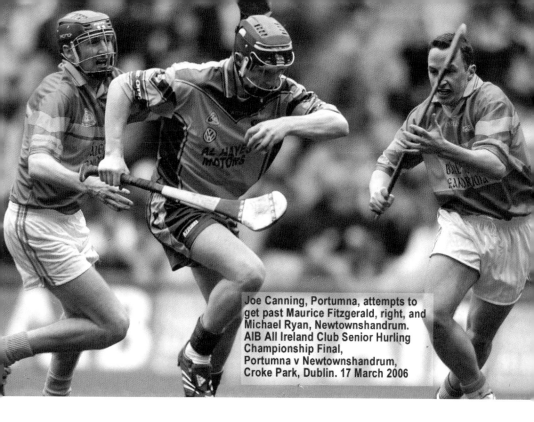

Joe Canning, Portumna, attempts to get past Maurice Fitzgerald, right, and Michael Ryan, Newtownshandrum. AIB All Ireland Club Senior Hurling Championship Final, Portumna v Newtownshandrum, Croke Park, Dublin. 17 March 2006

ALL IRELAND CLUB FINALS
A SPECIAL DAY FOR CLUBS

A very special day for the four clubs appearing in the finals, three of which are there for the first time.

Dublin's Connolly Station on Friday, March 17th, 2006 is a hive of activity. Men and women, young and old, hurry through the busy concourse; others linger there, relaxed and drinking tea or coffee.

Mobile phones continually bleep with the sound of text messages, the station is awash with colour as the AIB All Ireland club finals are in town. Everyone, it seems, is heading in the direction of Croke Park.

The colours brighten the gloom of a dull

March morning. The 'green and gold' of Cork champions Newtownshandrum, the 'blue and gold' of Galway standard bearers Portumna joined by their county colleagues in the 'blue, yellow and black' of Salthill-Knocknacarra.

There is an absence of 'blue and white' – that of St Gall's from Belfast, the majority of whom travelled down the M1 by various modes of transport.

As match time draws nearer, the station empties, but the booming voice on the sound system continues to give details for the return journey. Few if any take notice.

Supporters have more pressing matters to contend with.

Time was of course when St Patrick's Day was dominated by the Railway Cups in both codes, when the very best from the four provinces gathered to thrill thousands.

Then it was the deeds of Christy Ring, the Rackard brothers Nicky and Bobby, Sean Purcell, Mick O'Connell and Sean O'Neill that dominated the discussions for days after. However, as the saying goes 'time and tide waits for no man' and while the 'parade' and

'shamrock' are still an integral part of our national holiday, it's a day when the grassroots of the GAA, the club, commands centre stage.

It is a special day for the participating clubs who, with the exception of Newtownshandrum, are appearing in the finals for the very first time. It's an occasion that will live with them forever.

The next stop is Drumcondra Road, just a short distance from Croke Park. Here the supporters mingle freely, another great strength of the GAA – no need to segregate the fans.

As ever the 'craic' is mighty as they await the opening of the local hostelries. There is a need for liquid refreshment after the long journey and to fight off the cold. In fact, the games would suffer as a result of the elements on that cold St. Patrick's Day.

Time to move on. A look into the new Jury's Hotel directly opposite the stadium shows that it's packed to the rafters.

Once again it's a colourful scene with the various accents wafting through the air as supporters discuss the possible outcomes of the games which are fast approaching. The hotel staff of varied nationalities seem slightly bemused by it all, but they cope well.

Club final day is very different to the first and third Sundays in September. It's generally warmer in September, but this is a day for the loyal club supporter and they are here in strength.

It is also noticeable for the absence of 'touts' as tickets are plentiful and access to the stadium is easy. While the sound of 'apples, pears or chocolate' resonates through the air from stallholders, business is slow as many come well stocked with their own 'goodies'.

Suddenly attention is drawn to the sound of a fast approaching Garda motorcade with blue lights flashing and all eyes turn in its direction. It's a signal for the Portumna supporters to raise the decibel level higher again.

The coach carrying the Galway champions comes into view, flags and banners ruffle in the strong wind as the players, many of whom are listening to music on their personal stereos, wave and acknowledge their loyal following.

Others offer the clinched fist, as if to say 'we will not let you down'. Shortly they will be in the sanctuary of the dressing room as the throw-in time gets ever nearer.

Inside the stadium preparations continue. The stewards file into their match positions and are well wrapped up against the elements. All around the place is buzzing with anticipation of the drama that is about to unfold.

Upstairs in the warmer

Finian Hanley, Salthill / Knocknacarra, catches the ball ahead of Aodhan Gallagher, St Gall's. All Ireland Club Football Final, Croke Park, Dublin. 17 March 2006 surroundings of the hospitality suite, sponsors AIB are holding a reception for supporters of all four teams along with the members of the media in a relaxed and informal manner.

It's a pleasant way to while a way an hour before the gladiators enter the arena for the hurling decider. The hot food on offer is welcomed by all as is the warmth of the atmosphere.

By now it is 1.50pm. To a crescendo of noise, the men from Portumna appear from the dressing rooms at the Cusack Stand side of the stadium, followed a few minutes later by the champions of 2003, Newtownshandrum.

Referee Brian Gavin calls the respective captains together, Brendan Mulcahy from Newtownshandrum and Portumna's Eugene McEntee. Formalities completed, the game gets underway. It's the men from the West who have the advantage of the strong wind for the first half.

Within seven minutes, they have scored two goals – one from seventeen year old Joe Canning, who a few short weeks later sat his Leaving Certificate examination, but for now he has passed his first test with honours.

Newtown fight back and a wonder goal from Jerry O'Connor gives them hope as they trail by only five points at half-time, plus they will have the benefit of the wind in the second half.

In the respective dressing rooms, the coaches take over. Newtown's Bernie O'Connor tells his players to stick to the plan, work a bit harder and a second title will be yours.

Across the corridor Jimmy Heverin reassures his troops that the wind never won a match for anyone and the title is theirs if they really want it.

A few minutes later the teams prepare to re-enter the playing field. By now the crowd has swelled considerably. It eventually reaches 33,760, despite being the coldest St Patrick's Day in over eighty years.

There is a poignant moment in the Portumna dressing room. As the players leave, they touch a piece of paper pinned to the wall.

It contains the names and photographs of Keith Hayes and Joe O'Meara – two young players who tragically lost their lives in car accidents. They are remembered by all involved, who are determined to lift the trophy to honour their memory.

Thirty minutes later Portumna are champions thanks to a sterling second-half display that Newtown could not match. The full-time whistle is greeted by the now familiar pitch invasion. Despite the best efforts of the stewards and stadium officials, this is one march they are not going to stop.

After what seems an eternity, Eugene McEntee climbs the steps of the Hogan Stand where he is greeted by GAA President Sean Kelly, who pays tribute to Newtown for their wonderful effort and their contribution to a great final. He then hands the Tommy Moore Cup to a proud captain.

Eugene lifts it into the grey sky to the delight of what seems the entire town who are watching underneath, still on the hallowed turf.

It is the eighth time the cup will be heading to Galway. The trip across the Shannon is one they are looking forward to, if they ever get back to the safety of the dressing room to savour what they

have just achieved.

It's a hugely emotional time for the Hayes family, steeped in the tradition of the club and with the father's company as club sponsor. However, they all remember their brother and in a quiet moment a tear is shed by Damien and Niall, joy tinged with sadness.

Eventually the pitch is cleared to await the arrival of the footballers from St Gall's and Salthill-Knocknacarra. As with the hurling teams, they receive a rousing reception.

There is a widely held view that football is hard to watch after a hurling game as the pace is much slower. That opinion is re-inforced as this match fails to ignite.

Salthill hold the upper hand for long periods. With the sands of time running out, they lead by three points. St Gall's battle back and cut the lead to a single point and they have cause to regret a succession of bad wides.

The fourth official raises the board – three minutes to be added which is still enough time for the Ulster champions to force a replay. However, not for the first time, they turn over possession and when referee David Coldrick blows the full-time whistle, it is

Man of the match Joe Canning, centre, and Portumna captain Eugene McEntee, right, celebrate with the cup. All Ireland Club Hurling Championship Final, Portumna v Newtownshandrum, Croke Park, Dublin. 17 March 2006

Salthill-Knocknacarra who are crowned champions by the narrowest of margins.

The victors leap in the air with joy, the vanquished slump to the ground in agony. The journey home will be long and lonely as they ponder on what could have been had they taken their chances.

Once again hordes of supporters race to embrace their heroes who quickly console the men from the Falls Road.

The Andy Merrigan Cup is heading back to Galway but it's a Mayo man, Maurice Sheridan, who accepts it from Sean Kelly, who was denied the honour of presenting it to his namesake Sean Kelly, the St Gall's captain.

As he prepares to leave office, President Sean Kelly is about to present one of his last cups. Not for the first time, he introduces yet another angle to the proceedings.

1971 was the first year of the All

Ireland club championship. It was the brainchild of Bertie Coleman of Galway club Dunmore McHales. Bertie now joins the President on the podium as Sean Kelly pays tribute to him for his vision and foresight all those years ago.

It is somewhat ironic that the man whose club gave us the great competition it is today, looks on as a famous son of Dunmore McHales, Michael Donnellan, collects a winner's medal in the colours of Salthill-Knocknacarra.

The winners descend from the stand and are engulfed by their supporters; digital cameras capture the moment as the players accept the congratulations before retreating into the dressing rooms for their own quiet reflection on a momentous day.

Out on the field little groups stand together as the theme music from the Special Olympics booms across the emptying stadium. The stewards with gentle persuasion eventually clear the pitch and then are advised to stand down as another day is over.

Outside the dressing room, Salthill players and management are surrounded by reporters, microphones, dictaphones and mobile phones recording the quotes and comments that will make the following day's headlines.

Almost unnoticed, St Gall's players and mentors slip quietly away, heads bowed.

Darkness is slowly enveloping the stadium. However, back in the press area there is work still to be done.

Laptops and computers are punching out the details, quotes are fed into the system, notes checked and scorers recorded. A quick look out at the field, papers fluttering in the strong wind, seagulls swooping low in search of crumbs, as slowly but surely the day is drawing to a close.

Outside the stadium the cold of a March evening ensures not too many wait around. There is a long journey home to contend with, but the road west is a short one tonight.

For the first time since 1979, both titles are heading to the same county, as Galway standard bearers Portumna and Salthill-Knocknacarra are worthy AIB All Ireland club champions.

So the curtain falls on yet another outstanding club championship. The cups are

Sean Burns, St. Gall's, tries to get his kick away despite the attempted blocking by Brian Geraghty and Gordon Morley, right, Salthill / Knocknacarra. All Ireland Club Football Final, Croke Park, Dublin. 17 March 2006

leading back across the Shannon and the celebrations will continue long into the night and beyond.

Little did Bertie Coleman realise all those years ago what he was starting – from humble beginnings in 1971 to the biggest day in the life of any club and getting bigger.

No sooner has the dust settled on his year's campaign, when thoughts immediately turn to next season as clubs the length and breadth of the country strive to be in Croke Park on Lá Le Pádraig, for as Charles Kickham famously said 'the honour of the little village'.

We finish where we began, back in Connolly Station as the hordes of supporters begin the long

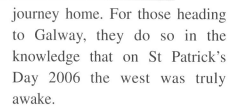
journey home. For those heading to Galway, they do so in the knowledge that on St Patrick's Day 2006 the west was truly awake.

For the record, the results of the AIB All Ireland Club Finals were:

Hurling
Portumna **2-8**
Newtownshandrum **1-6**

Football
Salthill-Knocknacarra . . . **0-7**
St Gall's **0-6**

Groundstaff attempt to clear the surface water from the pitch before the game. Dublin v Westmeath. Guinness Leinster Senior Hurling Championship, Quarter Final, O'Moore Park, Portlaoise, Co. Laois. 21 May 2006

MONSOON IN O'MOORE PARK

May 21st 2006 heralded the start of the Guinness Hurling Championships in both Leinster and Ulster. With the big guns still waiting in the wings, a low-key opening was expected. It was far from it. As former Taoiseach Albert Reynolds once said: 'it's the small things that trip you up'.

Dublin v Westmeath
Laois v Offaly

O'Moore Park, Portlaoise was the venue for a double-header in hurling and there was a degree of optimism that a good-sized crowd would attend. After all, Dublin had already won Division 2 of the league, Westmeath were the Christy Ring Cup holders and a local derby featuring Laois and Offaly was an attraction in itself.

Leinster Council officials must have felt the gods were against them when they

Offaly's Kevin Brady tries to gain possession on a waterlogged pitch in O'Moore Park. Laois v Offaly, Guinness Leinster Senior Hurling Championship, quarter final, O'Moore Park, Portlaoise, Co. Laois. 21 May 2006

looked out their windows early on Sunday morning. Grey, heavy skies were spitting rain and a strong wind was blowing at a ferocious rate – not a day for hurling.

The pitch was inspected twice at 10.30am and 12.30pm and declared playable, despite surface water appearing in certain areas. Ground staff worked hard in an effort to improve conditions for the players.

In truth they were fighting a losing battle as the wind and rain continued to batter the stadium and there was little sign of it relenting.

Elsewhere the weather was also taking its toll. The Connacht football game in Salthill – Sligo Galway – fell victim, which meant a two hour slot on RTÉ television was now vacant. A short distance from Portlaoise, the Irish Open Golf was taking place in Carton House. Such was the severity of the weather, play was abandoned there for the day.

Officials of the Leinster Council had the pitch inspected again prior to the first game – this time by match referee John Ryan. He once again deemed it playable.

The Dublin and Westmeath teams arrived at the venue to be informed that the game was on. Seamus Qualter, the Westmeath manager, insisted that the match should go ahead, feeling his team had a better chance in the conditions.

Dublin manager Tommy Naughton had no real opinion and would accept whatever decision was made.

It was also decided that there would be a further inspection after the first game to determine if the Laois v Offaly game could be played.

One particular area of the pitch was almost completely under water. In fact, Dublin corner-forward Kevin Flynn said it was like 'playing in a swamp'.

The game did start at the appointed time and while the rain eased for the first half, it made for an appalling spectacle as players battled in dreadful conditions. In the end, after enduring seventy minutes of hard slog in an almost deserted stadium, Westmeath emerged winners by 0-13 to 0-11. It was the first shock of the Hurling Championship.

The dilemma now was what would happen with the Laois v Offaly match. Due to the weather and the paltry attendance, those in the press contingent were certain it would be cancelled. It was not, and without consulting the respective managers, the game got under way. There is a view abroad that the need for live television played an important part in the decision to proceed.

By now the condition of the pitch had deteriorated further as the rain continued to pelt down on the sodden surface. Any attempt at good hurling was a waste of time. At the finish, Offaly were comfortable winners 2-12 to 0-8, but both managers were highly critical of the decision to play the game.

Dinny Cahill (Laois) and John McIntyre (Offaly) confirmed that neither was consulted. Had they been, they would have objected to proceeding with the game, both citing the safety of the players which should have been the first priority. Amazingly in the two games, despite the conditions,

A large puddle on the pitch before the game. Dublin v Westmeath, Guinness Leinster Senior Hurling Championship, quarter final, O'Moore Park, Portlaoise, Co. Laois. 21 May 2006

only one player, Philip Russell, from Laois was injured.

Cahill continued, 'it was the worst conditions I have ever experienced in all my years in hurling. That was league hurling out there and unfair on players who had trained hard all year to be asked to try and play on a day like today.'

McIntyre agreed and then added, 'it wasn't pretty but it was prettier than the Finnish group who won the Eurovision last night'. The fact that his team had just won may have lightened his mood somewhat.

With the small crowd long departed, it still meant a trip to the qualifiers for Dublin and Laois. Their Leinster Championship ambitions were submerged in the water that was still visible on the playing surface.

Monday dawned and the recriminations began. Conflicting views from the Leinster Council officers emerged.

Chairman Michael Delaney defended the decision to play the games, while Secretary Liam O'Neill disagreed.

A day later the GPA voiced their disapproval at the staging of the games. It said the decision showed scant regard for the welfare and well-being of the players who had made huge sacrifices and were treated shabbily by those who took the decision to play the games.

Photographs in many of the newspapers supported this view. The other question being asked was: would any of the leading counties, such as Cork, Kilkenny or Tipperary, be forced to play under such dreadful conditions?

A bad day all round in Portlaoise. And it must go down as an 'own goal' by the Leinster Council. It did little for the image of a Championship that has failed to capture the imagination of the public with several 'non events' in recent years. This debacle fits easily into that category.

Gaelic Park, The Bronx, New York. The scorekeeper adjusts the Down sign prior to the New York v Down, Ulster Senior Hurling Championship. 13 May 2001

VISA PROBLEMS FOR NEW YORK

Antrim v New York

On June 4th 2006, Ulster Hurling Final day, the playing fields of New York and Casement Park, Belfast, were silent – all because of a 'visa problem'.

It is fair to say that the Ulster Hurling Championship, with all due respect to the participants, carries little appeal. With only five counties involved, it is easy to see why. However, this year's Championship made the headlines, all of them unwanted.

In the first round, Antrim as expected defeated London and then accounted for Down in the semi final. It was all going according to plan so far. Now all that was required was for

Derry to beat New York in the other semi final in the 'Big Apple'.

But this is where the story really began.

It finished New York 1-18 Derry 1-12, and major celebrations began amongst the hard-working GAA folk in New York. It was a thoroughly deserved win with Michael 'Bonny' Kennedy contributing 1-7 of his side's total.

After the general euphoria of the win abated, reality dawned on New York GAA officials. Could they play the final fixed for Casement Park, Belfast on Sunday June 4th?

In fact, two days after the win over Derry, the New York GAA Board informed the Ulster Council they would not be in a position to play the final on the date scheduled. Officially, Chairman Seamus Dooley said logistically it would be 'impossible for us to arrange for a party of 40 or 50 to travel to Ireland in the time allowed with work commitments and

everything else; we would need at least four weeks'.

Pointedly, he then added that people should appreciate our reluctance to travel, 'everyone knows the reason why'. This was taken as a clear reference to the legal status of individuals and the potential threat to their livelihoods.

The Ulster Council refused to comment other than to acknowledge that New York had requested a postponement. Initially, Antrim were saying very little, although their secretary Jim Murray said, 'we will await direction from the Ulster Council'.

Kevin Kennedy, New York in action against John Caughey, Down. New York v Down, Ulster Senior Hurling Championship. 3 June 2000

These events failed to put a damper on the celebrations in New York. Seamus Dooley said, 'people are celebrating as if we had won an All Ireland, we had great craic and the atmosphere was wonderful. It is a marvellous boost to the game in the city. We trained hard since January so we were confident of winning. We even told the Ulster Council we would win.'

With the certainty that their request for a postponement would be denied, New York offered to pay for flights and accommodation for Antrim if they agreed to travel to New York or indeed Boston to fulfil the fixture.

Dooley explained, 'it's a huge game for us and it would be a massive blow for New York hurling if it didn't go ahead because there is a chance of something historic happening'.

As expected, the Ulster Council, at a special meeting attended by Seamus Dooley, refused to defer the final because in the words of Secretary Danny Murphy 'fixtures are set at the start of the year and there is a logic and schedule behind them'.

He also ruled out the possibility of playing it later in the year, saying 'Antrim are involved in the Christy Ring Cup and are expected to make the final. If we played the Ulster final after the Championship it would belittle the competition. We are sympathetic to New York's plight but they were aware of the fixtures from early in the year.'

It should be noted that Antrim opted out of the race for the Liam McCarthy Cup preferring to concentrate on the Christy Ring Cup for second tier counties. The reward for winning was a trip to New York or Boston for the winners. But they got an early shock in their bid for glory in this competition.

Antrim too were disappointed at the prospect of the final being abandoned, as they stood on the brink of a fifth successive title. Star forward Brian McFall admitted it was now unlikely to take place. 'It's a shame as we would love to play the game, but time is running out.'

By now it appeared as if all avenues to play the final in New York had been explored. The likelihood was that the final would be abandoned. New York manager Monty Moloney let rip at Antrim's attitude.

Gaelic Park, The Bronx, New York.

In an interview with Simon Lewis of the *Irish Examiner*, he branded them 'cowards'. 'They're cowards straight out,' he blasted, 'they're running scared because when they came out here last year they got a fright and it needed the referee to send off three of our fellas before they got past us.'

Moloney also ridiculed the suggestion that an August date would pose scheduling problems. 'This is not the 1940s we are talking about. They can come out here for a weekend as many teams do and still be back in work on Monday. If they are as good as they say they are, why can't they come out and play?'

A clearly angry Moloney continued, 'don't be afraid, don't be hiding and don't be using this as an excuse. They are hiding behind the fact that they have the title, it's as clear as day.'

In a final blast he took another swipe at what he calls the patronising attitude adopted by Antrim. 'When they were coming over and beating us every year we were the best in the world. Now all of a sudden we've got a team that can take them on and it's a totally different story.'

Harsh words indeed from a man who has devoted a lifetime of service to the GAA in New York. At times it has been hard, very hard and it's a pity that they were denied their possible hour of glory.

On what should have been a momentous occasion for the hurlers of New York, the playing fields in the 'Big Apple' and Casement Park, Belfast were silent on Ulster Hurling Final day June 4th, all because of a 'visa problem'.

Due to the failure to play the final, Antrim were declared champions. This has cast major doubts on New York's future participation in both the Ulster Hurling and Connacht Football Championships. As it is quite clear under the current circumstances, this problem is not going to go away.

Note:
The Ulster Hurling Final was eventually scheduled to take place in Boston on 22 October to coincide with the Martin Donnelly-sponsored Inter-Provincial Football Final.

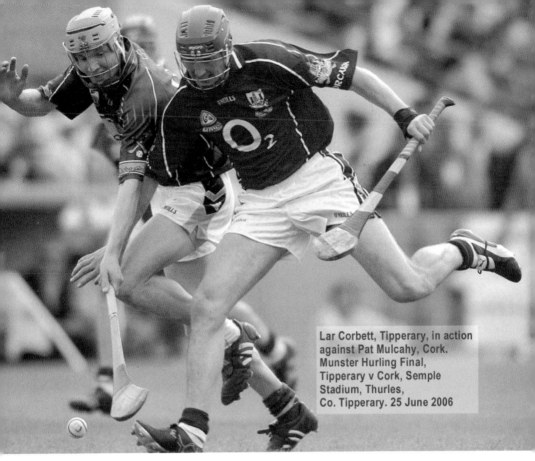

Lar Corbett, Tipperary, in action against Pat Mulcahy, Cork. Munster Hurling Final, Tipperary v Cork, Semple Stadium, Thurles, Co. Tipperary. 25 June 2006

The Munster Hurling Final

Cork v Tipperary

In the immediate aftermath of their semi final win over Waterford, Tipperary manager Babs Keating remarked, 'Cork and Tipperary in the Munster hurling final is special'.

Babs should know – as a player and manager

he has been involved in so many finals, they (or more importantly the result) very often define his year.

June 25th, 2006 was no different. It was a warm morning as various modes of transport headed to Thurles from Cork, a journey that all 'rebel' supporters relish. Trains too were full to capacity while Tipperary supporters made their way to the cathedral town for a meeting with the 'old enemy'.

The clash evokes memories of bygone days and the deeds of so many outstanding hurlers spring to mind. The names of Ring, Doyle, Lynch, Stakelum, Nealon, Barry Murphy, Cummins and English regularly crop up, but for the younger generation it's a different set of heroes.

Kelly, 'Redser' and Cummins for Tipperary; Ben and Jerry, Corcoran, Sully and Deano for Cork. These are the names that now capture the imagination.

Liberty Square in Thurles was a sea of colour and with Cork and Tipperary also in the minor final, four colours dominated: 'blue and gold' and 'red and white'. For the next few hours, the happenings in the world were put to one side. All that matters was the result of the Guinness Munster Hurling Final. The scene was set, let the battle commence.

En route to the final, Tipperary recorded wins over Limerick and Waterford, showing improvement in each outing and relishing the challenge the champions would present. Cork had an easy win over Clare who faded badly after a bright opening 20 minutes. Cork are favourites, but form goes out the window when it comes to a Cork v Tipp Munster final.

There was the added responsibility on both counties to produce a good game. It had been a mediocre Championship up to this point and fans hoped the age old rivals would not disappoint. The other ingredient in the mix was the form of Tipp's Eoin Kelly, whose talent had been the one spark in the Championship to date. In the games against Limerick and Waterford he amassed a total score of 2-23. The question being asked was how would Cork contain the Mullinahone man. The task of curbing Kelly was handed to Cork's Brian Murphy. Another little cameo in a fascinating contest.

Cork fans cheer on their side while Tipperary fans cheer on their county during the Munster Hurling Final, Tipperary v Cork, Semple Stadium, Thurles, Co. Tipperary. 25 June 2006

In keeping with tradition, the curtain raiser was the ESB minor final [Cork v Tipperary]. It was first blood to Cork with a decisive 2-20 to 1-15 – a three-in-a-row for the 'young rebels' and a boost for the seniors.

The tension in the stadium was now palpable as the attendance of 53,268 awaited the arrival of the teams. Red and white dominated the town end of the ground, while it was blue and gold at the Killinan End, with a liberal sprinkling of red and white.

It was a special day too for groundsman Jimmy Purcell, who was overseeing his last Munster final as he retires in a short few months. Would he sign off with a win for his beloved Tipperary? He would get his answer in the next 90 minutes.

Stunning start by Tipperary

Experienced referee Dickie Murphy called the captains. Formalities complete, the game got underway. It was Tipperary who made the better start. In the very first attack, Diarmuid Fitzgerald got in behind the Cork defence and only the brilliance of goalkeeper Donal Óg Cusack denied him a certain goal. It was at the expense of a '65' which Eoin Kelly pointed.

Three minutes later the Cork defence was breached again. This time Cusack was powerless to prevent Lar Corbett drilling the ball to the net. The challengers could not have asked for a better start – 1-1 on the board and Cork yet to score.

However, this Cork team has built a vast reservoir of experience in their climb to the top in recent years. Panic is not in their vocabulary. The game settles down, so does the Cork defence, helped by the dominance of their half-back line.

Jerry O'Connor gets a Cork point, quickly followed by a brace of points from Joe Deane. It was noticeable also that Brian Murphy was coping with Kelly, winning the first few tussles. A nice confidence boost for the Bride Rovers man.

Cork's first goal arrived on 12 minutes. Deane and Brian Corcoran combined for Corcoran to score his sixth goal in Championship hurling. Cork are in front 1-3 to 1-1, and Tipp's early fire seems extinguished. By the 18th minute, both sides have added two points each. Even though they were playing against the breeze, Tipperary would have been happy at the direction the game was going.

Two minutes later they were dealt a hammer blow with a trademark Cork goal. It all began with Brian Murphy beating Eoin Kelly in a race for possession, then setting in train a sequence of passes that would not have been out of place in the World Cup in Germany. It was the new Cork, passing and running to perfection, with the Tipperary defence being ripped apart.

Ben O'Connor, Ronan Curran, Timmy McCarthy and Tom Kenny were all involved, before Kenny's defence-splitting pass found O'Connor in acres of space. Ben picked his spot and fired an unstoppable shot past Brendan Cummins for a goal of real quality. It put Cork 2-5 to 1-3 ahead.

The goal galvanised Tipperary and they went on to enjoy their most productive period in what was now developing into a gripping contest. In the next 13 minutes, they scored seven points, four from placed balls by Eoin Kelly, who was making little headway against the tenacious Murphy. The other scorers were Paul Kelly, who was doing well in midfield, and John O'Brien.

Cork's only reply was a long range effort from John Gardiner. It meant that at the break it was all square.

No doubt it was Babs who was the happier of the two managers as they headed for the dressing room. Level with the champions and the breeze to favour Tipperary in the second half. Little wonder then that the Tipp supporters were in buoyant mood as they contemplated a first Championship win over their arch rivals since 1991.

Crucially Cork got the first two points of the second half – both scored from frees by Joe Deane, who was fast eclipsing Eoin Kelly as the most effective forward in the game.

John Carroll, who had a good outing on Sean Óg Ó'hAilpín, and Brian Corcoran traded points, before Eoin Kelly brought the sides level again, with two points, including one point, his only one at that, from play.

Cork though were gaining control as their half-back line of John Gardiner, Ronan Curran and Sean Óg kept a vice-like grip on their opposite numbers. It had the effect of limiting supply to the inside line and in particular to Kelly.

In fact, two of the three Tipp half forwards, including team captain Redser O'Grady were replaced. Tom Kenny thundered into the game in midfield and Shane McGrath impressed for Tipperary. Paul Kelly's lack of match fitness saw him leave the action early.

Cork too had their problems in attack. Like Tipperary, two of their three half-forwards were called ashore, but their difficulties were not as pronounced as Tipperary's. It was clear once Kelly was held, Tipp would struggle for scores. Indeed scores were scarce in the second half. Tipperary only managed five points despite playing with the breeze.

Cork fans Emma and Darragh Newman and Eadaoin Farrell mingling with Tipperary fans

Deane edged Cork ahead again with two fabulous points from play in the 49th and 51st minutes. The chant of 'Deano Deano' rang out from the masses on the terracing behind the goal as the white flag was raised by the umpire.

However, Tipperary were still in touch. The fact that they never actually took the lead, apart from Corbett's goal in the third minute, was crucial.

Deane and Corbett exchanged points and then Tipperary substitute Benny Dunne landed a great score four minutes from time. Now in the great tradition that is the Munster Final, only one point divided the teams.

Tipperary had a chance to draw level, but Eoin Kelly could not shake off Murphy. In fact, twice in quick succession he was blocked down. On the one occasion in which he did manage to get a shot on target, it was stopped by Cusack. With it went Tipperary's last chance of saving the game. From the resultant clearance, the ball broke in midfield to Cork substitute Kieran Murphy and with his first touch he landed a massive point. Cork were two points in front and now only a goal could save the home side. It never really looked like coming.

As the board signalling three minutes of added time was raised, Cork once again repelled a Tipperary attack and won a free at the other end. Fittingly, Joe Deane converted it, and now the champions could breathe easy – a three point gap and the sands of time running out.

The game ended with Cork still pressing for another score. As the dust rose in the Tipperary square, reminiscent of days gone by and 'hell's kitchen', the full-time whistle sounded. Cork were champions for the 50th time at the end of a titanic battle for supremacy on a 2-14 to 1-14 scoreline.

It was a typical Munster final with many outstanding displays, most of them in defence. For Cork, the players wearing numbers 1 to 7 reaffirmed again their status as the best in the business, while Paul Curran and Paul Ormonde were excellent for Tipperary.

Joe Deane won the battle of the number 15s hands down, but Eoin Kelly would inflict further damage on opposing defenders before the season has run its course.

The aftermatch reaction was neatly summed up by Tipperary manager Babs Keating, who said 'there is a lot of hurling to be played yet and if we can learn from today we will be a better team as a result'.

Cork boss John Allen, while delighted to win, was disappointed with some aspects of his team's play. 'It is always great to win the Munster Championship especially in Thurles, but we will need to look at some of our play as it was poor at times, but having said that we are now Munster champions and we move on from here to the next phase of the season.'

So the curtain comes down on yet another chapter in the fabled story that is the Munster final. For the time being at least, it was the sound of 'De Bank's' that

reverberated around the famous old stadium. But it is only June and under the present format do not rule out the men from the 'Valley of Slievenamon' having a

say in the destination of hurling's greatest prize as the months roll on.

Cork	....	2-14
Tipperary	....	1-14

The Kilkenny players stand for the National Anthem. Wexford v Kilkenny, Leinster Senior Hurling Final, Croke Park. 2 July 2006

LEINSTER HURLING CHAMPIONSHIP

A ONE HORSE RACE?

The Leinster Hurling Championship has failed to produce any surprising results in recent years. Would 2006 be the year to buck this trend?

Unlike its counterpart in Munster, the Guinness Leinster Hurling Championship badly needs a lift. There is a lack of atmosphere before and after the final, with the presentation of the Bob O'Keeffe cup very often taking place in an almost deserted stadium. This year was no exception as Kilkenny's Jackie Tyrell became the eighth captain in nine years from the Marble County to lift the cup.

For years a Kilkenny v Wexford final held its own appeal, but then along came Offaly to add another important dimension to an ailing and aged pairing.

The Dooleys, Pilkingtons, Johnny Flaherty and Pat Delaney were a breath of fresh air to a championship that benefited from an infusion of new blood. They came, saw and conquered and for a 15-year period were a force to be reckoned with. In fact, Offaly contested 11 successive Leinster finals. In the same period they won their first Liam McCarthy Cup, added two more in time and gave hope to the rest that the Cork, Kilkenny, Tipperary triumvirate could be broken. At last a new county was emerging.

contains Laois, Dublin and Westmeath. The more salient point is that Kilkenny have moved further ahead of the rest, as the following facts will testify: 15 of the last 17 minor titles and 11 of the last 15 under-21 titles have found a resting place in the county. It looks as if Kilkenny's dominance is set to continue for some time yet.

Wexford won the All Ireland in 1996 and were defeated by Tipperary in the semi final in 1997. Since then only one Leinster title – in 2004 – has found its way to the Model County. The graph in Wexford is also on a downward spiral with under-age titles a rarity for the county.

The result is that for many, the Leinster hurling championship is seen as a one-horse race with Kilkenny in a class of their own.

Rory Jacob, Wexford on the attack against Offaly. Leinster Hurling, Semi Final, Offaly v Wexford, Nowlan Park, Kilkenny. 11 June 2006

Gradually though, the lack of adequate replacements took its toll. Offaly have slipped back into the pack that

It is also the principal reason why Kilkenny place great emphasis on the National League. Simply put, they need good quality games to keep them sharp for the tougher tests that lie ahead.

This year's championship got off to the worst possible start with the O'Moore Park weather debacle and in truth it never really recovered.

The semi finals are normally on the same day in Croke Park but this year they were played separately as HQ was unavailable because of a Robbie Williams concert. Kilkenny travelled to Cusack Park in Mullingar to play revitalised Westmeath. Although the home side were competitive, there was always only going to be one winner.

Wexford and Offaly met in the second semi final before a very good attendance in Nowlan Park, Kilkenny – a perfect setting for what should have been a good game. However, the match was a dour and listless affair and despite the closeness of the score (Wexford won 0-9 to 0-8), the game did little to lift the championship. The question now being asked was, how many would actually attend the final in Croke Park.

Due to the inclusion of the delayed Wexford v Offaly football semi final, a crowd of 44,476 attended, guaranteeing a decent atmosphere, especially with Wexford doubly involved. The downside of this schedule saw the Carlow minor hurlers on their first ever appearance in a Leinster final playing Kilkenny at 12.30 before a few thousand spectators.

Kilkenny v Wexford

It had been a very poor year at senior level for Wexford and the squad was beset with problems as several key players for a variety of reasons opted out. Yet if they were at full strength they had a chance, as Kilkenny themselves were in the words of Brian Cody 'in transition'.

It was their first final since DJ Carey's retirement while other key players of recent years, such as Peter Barry and John Hoyne, had also departed the scene. Even so, the pundits and experts could only see one winner.

It was a very poor decider. The crowd, apart from a brief period just after half-time, were rarely involved, such was the paucity of Wexford's challenge.

The champions made an excellent start and rattled over three points in the opening six minutes as Wexford struggled to cope with the pace and power of Kilkenny's hurling. That they did not score more was down to poor shooting and dogged resistance from the challengers. In fact Wexford at one stage drew level but they were unable to sustain their challenge.

Kilkenny were always in control. A cracking goal from Henry Shefflin helped them to the interval lead of 1-9 to 0-4 and only one Wexford forward Rory Jacob had scored from play in the first 35 minutes. Wexford did little for their chances by omitting Michael Jacob from the starting line up. On his introduction for the second half he helped himself to 1-4, all from play, and when you consider Wexford's total was only 2-12 it made his omission all the more baffling.

In fact, within seven minutes of the resumption Wexford had doubled their tally, to 0-8, and they were further boosted when Rory Jacob got their first goal.

By now the gap was down to three points. There was an expectation that the game would finally spring to life. Kilkenny had dropped their earlier intensity and were sluggish. But the Wexford revival was quickly nipped in the bud by a Kilkenny side who, sensing the danger, upped the tempo.

In defence, Jackie Tyrell and Tommy Walsh (named man of the match) came into their own, aided by a number of important substitutions. These changes helped produce six points in a ten-minute period. Were it not for a vital interception by Wexford defender Malachy Travers, Kilkenny's Eoin Larkin would have had a goal.

It was the end of the game as a meaningful contest. Long before the finish many in the crowd had lost interest in the proceedings. Only the brief appearance of a streaker helped liven matters up during a boring second half. Michael Jacob's goal in injury time was greeted with barely a ripple of applause and only served to take the bare look off the scoreboard. Kilkenny were comfortable winners by 1-23 to Wexford's 2-12.

A 63rd senior title then for the 'Cats' and once again the debate began surrounding the current state of the Leinster championship and how to improve a competition that Kilkenny currently dominates.

One suggestion frequently mooted is the inclusion of Galway in the Leinster Championship. It is believed that the Hurling Development Committee discussed this matter at a meeting in the week of the Leinster Final. With the structures of the hurling championship to be reviewed at the end of the current campaign, it is bound to surface again.

It was first raised in 2003 but the Galway clubs voted a resounding 'no' in October of that year.

Even now though it seems the possibility of Galway joining Leinster is as far away as ever, if the comments of the provincial chairman Liam O'Neill are any indication.

O'Neill in an interview within 48 hours of the final said 'those people who are mooting this suggestion would need to engage with Leinster and put a package together that was going to make it worth our while'.

The first priority of the Leinster council he continued, 'is to the Leinster counties and not to provide Galway with an extra

Kilkenny captain Jackie Tyrell celebrates with the cup at the end of the Leinster Hurling Final, Wexford v Kilkenny, Croke Park, Dublin. 2 July 2006

game; a situation could develop where you would have a Galway v Kilkenny final in every grade every year. What benefit would that be?'

The Chairman stressed the amount of good work going on in the province at the moment: 'remember Dublin won last year's (2005) minor title and Carlow reached this year's final and with the ongoing development work the situation could change in the coming years, but there is little doubt that right now Kilkenny are just too good for the rest'.

His final comment would seem to put an end to all talk of Galway joining the championship: 'the Galway idea should be shelved and the comprehensive hurling plan currently in place needs to be fine tuned and in time the benefits will be seen'.

Is it then a case of 'Leinster says no to Galway?' Maybe, but in any case the championship is in serious danger of becoming a non-event and needs a revamp and quickly. It could best be said that

what began as a damp squib in Portlaoise on May 21st finished in a damp squib in Croke Park on July 2nd.

Now a last word on the final and let's finish on a brighter note. In the 1979 final, Wexford met Kilkenny and the referee was Gerry Kirwan from Offaly. Twenty-seven years later his son Diarmuid officiated at this year's decider between the same counties. Kilkenny won it in 1979 and they won it again in 2006 – some things rarely change!

Na Piarsaigh captain Keith Buckley lifts the Christy Ring cup after winning the Hurling Final to become Féile Champions 2006. 18 June 2006

Féile na nGael
A Festival of Hurling

In 1971 three men sat down to discuss how hurling could be promoted nationally. Thirty five years later their idea is one of the most prestigious events in the GAA calendar.

Tipperary in the spring of 1971: Three men with a lifelong interest in the GAA and specifically in hurling sit down and discuss how the game could be promoted on a national basis. It was an informal chat, but as the evening wore on the discussion evolved. Out of it came Féile na nGael. Thirty-five years later it is one of the most prestigious events in the Association's calendar.

It is often said that the best ideas are the simplest ones. This is a perfect example of how simplicity works.

Seamus Ó'Riain, Tommy Barrett and Eamonn Stafford are the three men who first conceived the idea of Féile – a 'Festival of Hurling' for young boys under the age of 15. Since then, it has expanded to encompass camogie and handball with the age group reduced to under 14.

With the passing of time, the competition has grown in stature. For many a young boy and girl, it is very often the highlight of their sporting career.

Seamus Ó'Riain is a former president of the GAA. His profile and genuine love of hurling helped convince the Tipperary GAA people to run with the idea.

The central issue was to invite one juvenile team from each of the 31 other counties to Tipperary to compete over a weekend against 32 teams from the parishes of the county. I suppose it could well be described as the original 'trip to Tipp'.

The visiting teams would be hosted by the clubs in Tipperary that they would play against, thus forging new friendships that in many cases have been maintained to this day. It also helped reduce the cost factor. Coca-Cola came on board as sponsors and they are still there today.

Jimmy Smyth, a former Clare hurler and a prominent GAA official in Croke Park, was contacted to see if he would like to be involved. He immediately offered his support.

Apart from the hurling, other events were organised by various subcommittees to coincide with Féile. Many of these are still in place today, as the 2006 competition rolled into Cork on the third weekend in June.

The history of the competition is littered with the names of young boys and girls who went on to carve out outstanding careers in hurling and camogie at the highest level.

Davy Fitzgerald, Pete Finnerty, Sean Óg Ó'hAilpín and Michael Duignan are just some of these names. Their boyish looks on the cover of the 2006 programme is testimony to their contribution.

The late and great Christy Ring also had an affinity with the competition. In 1976, Cork was the venue and his son Christy Jnr was on the Glen Rovers team that won the title. The man who won eight All Ireland medals could be seen exhorting his beloved Glen to victory in every game.

It is only fitting then that the Division 1 trophy is called after the game's greatest exponent. On his death in 1979, his former colleagues in Shell Ireland donated the trophy to the Féile Committee. It depicts the 'Tower of Cloyne', the hurling mad village where Christy came from in East Cork.

When the first competition was won in 1971 (Blackrock from Cork were the winners) plans were immediately put in place to make it an annual event. What we have today is a tribute to those men of vision whose idea it was all those years ago.

Preparatory work begins early each year at both club and county level and anticipation levels rise as the day of reckoning arrives.

In 2006, a couple of months in advance of the competition, visits to schools by GAA President Nickey Brennan and Camogie President Liz Howard are arranged. They are accompanied by hurling and camogie players from Cork and are warmly greeted as they spread the word – Féile Na nGael is in town and it's a show not to be missed.

Registration forms must be filled in, Féile officials at all venues have to be appointed, fixtures schedules must be drawn up, referees need to be selected, and of course the Féile parade has to be organised. Anxious moments come and go but Friday June 16th finally arrives and the sun is shining brightly in the clear blue sky. Perfect.

It could well be described as

'moving day', because from early morning buses depart from the four corners of the country all with one destination in mind, Cork. Teams also travel from London and Warwickshire.

Thankfully all 178 hurling and camogie teams arrive safely in the 'Rebel County'. Once the initial greetings by the host clubs are complete, it's down to business.

Tradition dictates that the hosts play their visitors in the opening game on a Friday afternoon. The bulk of the games then take place on Saturday.

Friday night is Parade Night and a wonderful and colourful sight it is as the streets of Cork City belong to the young boys and girls from Ireland and beyond.

Union Quay is the assembly point and it is a hive of activity as the parade order is checked and rechecked. The famed Artane Band head the parade to the cheers of hundreds of people lining the route.

Dublin as hurling winners in 2005 and Cork as camogie winners lead the parade, with the club banners gently blowing in the warm summer breeze. At the appointed time of 7.30pm, the parade begins. It passes a reviewing stand containing the various dignitaries. As a memento of their visit to Cork, each captain receives a commerative pennant from Nickey Brennan and Liz Howard.

As it reaches the reviewing stand, Micheál Ó'Muireartaigh introduces each team and quickly mentions the many stars of bygone days who accompany them.

Pat Horgan with Glen Rovers, Michael Walsh with Dicksboro, Brian Donnelly with Ballycastle and surely the proudest of them all is legendary former Tipperary star Pat Stakelum with Durlas óg.

After a short speech of welcome by Nickey Brennan, the teams disperse. There are important games to be played on Saturday, the results of which will determine the fate of many in Féile 2006.

Saturday June 17

Another glorious sunny morning, perfect hurling weather. It's 10am at the many well appointed venues throughout the county and the action gets underway. The Féile office is based in Páirc Uí Rinn where a bank of phones are silent but not for long. The officials arrive and glance at the watches Shortly now the first results wil

Catríona Mackey, Douglas, and Rosie O'Mahoney, Inniscarra, compete in the Division 1 Camogie Final, Féile na nGael, Páirc Uí Rinn, Cork. 18 June 2006.

filter through. At 10.45am, the silence of the room is shattered as the phones begin to ring. For the next twenty minutes officials concentrate on taking down the exact score of each game. A point misplaced could be costly. It sets the trend for the rest of the day. These experienced officials quickly sense who will emerge from the groups. Immediately, thoughts turn to the possible pairings for the knockout stages as venues and referees need to be confirmed.

By 2pm, all the group games are concluded. There are one or two hitches along the way but generally everything runs smoothly. A minor discipline issue needs to be resolved. National Chairman Jim Berry and Secretary Jerome Conway summon the parties to Páirc Uí Rinn. A small subcommittee is on stand-by. They assemble, hear the evidence, issue findings, job done, move on.

It is now fast approaching 3pm and the lads involved in the skills competition gather on the lush surface of Páirc Uí Rinn. There are 19 participants in all, and the searing heat does not help.

At the end of a fascinating hour in which the very best of the skills of hurling are displayed, Niall Arthur from Inagh in County Clare is declared the winner – a weekend to remember for one young lad at least.

During the day Nickey Brennan and Liz Howard visit as many venues as possible to thank those who are working so hard to ensure the weekend is a success.

Nickey's mode of transport is a helicopter. He hopes it will be used again when the Féile goes to Kilkenny in 2007.

It is now mid afternoon and after a brief respite the phones begin to hop again as the results of the quarter finals start to reach the office. Thankfully they all work out and the stage is set for the semi finals which are due to begin at 7.30pm.

It's been a long day. Coca-Cola, water, tea and sandwiches are dispensed at a furious rate as the officials await the results that will shape Sunday's programme.

A long day too for the players and mentors, as they experience every strand of emotion before their fate is determined.

For some it's an early exit which means a stress-free afternoon, for others it is a frustrating few hours as the months and weeks of preparation hinges on 20 minutes of hurling. A bad miss, a poor clearance or even a controversial decision could make or break a team's weekend.

Eventually when the dust settles and the sun sinks behind the clouds around 9pm, 20 teams are left to contest the Féile Finals of 2006. For the other teams, their dreams and ambitions are over for another year.

Teams not involved can now relax as receptions are laid on in all clubs. Presentations are given and speeches of welcome and praise are made, while boys and girls exchange mobile phone numbers with a promise to keep in touch.

The night slowly slips into the next day, most oblivious to the hour, such is the convivial nature of the surroundings. In many respects, it is what Féile na nGael is all about.

Sunday June 18 – Finals' day
The day of reckoning is at hand. Unfortunately the glorious

weather of the previous two days gives way to wind and rain.

With 10 finals to be played, it means a tight schedule. The presence of Setanta Sports cameras in Páirc Uí Rinn adds to the occasion.

The stadium itself is in immaculate condition. The flags of the 32 participating counties are proudly displayed, as well as the flags of the 4 provinces and the GAA flag.

A similar picture can be seen in Páirc Uí Chaoimh where the action gets underway at 10am.

The honour of being the first winners of the day belongs to Sarsfields camogie team from Cork who beat Rathoath from Meath by 5-0 to 4-0 in the Division 4 Final.

In the Division 6 hurling final, Butlerstown from Waterford defeat Croke Rovers from Cork. There is glory for Cloyne, the home club of Donal Óg Cusack and Diarmuid O'Sullivan, as they annex the Division 5 title with a good victory over Kerry representatives Kenmare/Kilgarvan.

Another win for Waterford in Division 3 camogie as Lismore prove too strong for Newtownshandrum, and with that the action in Páirc Uí Chaoimh is complete.

Focus now is on Páirc Uí Rinn as the crowds gather for the big hurling and camogie finals.

Ulster teams are to the fore and the hard-working hurling people get ready to battle for victory.

Glenarriffe Oisin from Antrim just edge out Donoughmore from Cork to claim the Division 4 title and it sets in train joyous scenes of celebration. St John's from Belfast make it a double with a great win

Ciara Lynch, Douglas, celebrates her club's victory as Camogie President Liz Howard looks on. 18 June 2006.

Christopher Joyce, Na Piarsaigh, keeps the ball ahead of him during the Division 1 Hurling Final, Páirc Uí Rinn, Cork. 18 June 2006.

over Blarney from Cork to take the Division 2 honours.

A third Antrim team contest the Division 3 hurling final and it pits Ballycastle against Naas from Kildare. There is no joy though for the boys from the Glens of Antrim who lose by 6-6 to 1-5.

The Naas team is coached by Peter O'Hehir, son of the legendary Míceal O'Hehir whose grandson Conor is the team captain, a tradition maintained.

Eight down and two to go. The tension is mounting as the time is fast approaching for the Division 1 finals in hurling and camogie.

Before that though it's an all-Ulster final in Division 2 camogie, Ballinscreen from Derry against Ballycran from Down.

It's nail biting stuff for both sets of supporters. Mothers, fathers, brothers, sisters, friends and practically everyone from the respective clubs endure a torrid 40 minutes.

They shout, roar, bite nails, turn away and go through every emotion. In the end, Ballycran win by the narrowest of margins: 1-2 to 1-1.

The trophy presentation is heartbreak for Ballinscreen as their captain Catherine McNamee, overcome by emotion, introduces her players – many in tears – to camogie President Liz Howard. Not even a consoling word from Liz or a hug from her mother could help Catherine contain her emotions.

Eventually, Ballycran's captain Suzelle Johnson steps forward to accept the cup and pays tribute to Ballinscreen for a wonderful contest.

Next up are the camogie players of Douglas and Inniscarra in the

Division 1 decider. This is an all-Cork affair with Douglas bidding for a third successive title. The champions get the perfect start with two goals from full-forward Jessica Kavanagh. It leaves Inniscarra with a mountain to climb and it proves beyond them as Douglas stay in control and complete the three-in-a-row.

A special day too for 11 year old Claire Shine – a name and a player for the future.

The stage is now set for the Division 1 hurling final with the Christy Ring trophy on offer. Na Piarsaigh from Cork and St Mary's Athenry from Galway will vie for the ultimate honour – Féile champions 2006.

Na Piarsaigh are favourites and start in blistering fashion. A goal from inspirational captain Keith Buckley helps them to an interval lead of 1-5 to 0-3.

The Galway lads get the perfect boost early in the second half when Conor Caulfield fires in a cracking goal.

It develops into a fascinating contest as both sides give it their all, but weary limbs of the young lads show signs of a hectic weekend's activity.

St Mary's come at Na Piarsaigh in wave after wave of attack but their defence stands firm. Conor Caulfield gets a late point but it is not enough to deny Na Piarsaigh a sixth title, as they win by 1-5 to 1-4.

For the last time on a memorable day Nickey Brennan makes the presentation to a winning captain as the famous trophy in honour of the greatest hurler of them all is set to reside in the Northside of Cork city for the next 12 months.

So Féile 2006 is finally over and all who contributed to its success on and off the field can reflect on a job very well done.

The visitors leave Cork with happy memories of their stay on Leeside and over the long winter months they will recall the highs and lows of three days of fantastic action.

218 hurling games played, not one red card shown and only three yellow cards, 140 camogie matches with every team epitomising what Féile is all about.

Roll on June 2007 when the hurling folk of Kilkenny will play host to Féile na nGael.

The Cork and Kerry teams march behind the Artane Boys' band in the pre-match parade before the game, with a backdrop of the Macgillicuddy Reeks. Kerry v Cork, Munster Football Final, Fitzgerald Stadium, Killarney, Co. Kerry. 9 July 2006

The MUNSTER Football Final
Battle in Beauty's home

Cork v Kerry in a Munster Football Final. No surprise there – but these two teams can produce fantastically exciting football when they clash.

Kerry v Cork

It is called, and rightly so, the most scenic venue in Gaelic games – Fitzgerald Stadium, Killarney. When Cork and Kerry clash in the Munster football final, there is no better place to be.

The stadium is unique in that it has only one stand. The rest of the picturesque ground is terraced. When full to capacity there isn't many better sights, apart from the 'hill' when the Dubs are playing in Croke Park.

The press box is situated opposite the main stand. With the cathedral spire and the Macgillycuddy Reeks in the background, it provides the perfect setting for an eagerly awaited contest.

The Munster Football Championship, if not exactly a one-horse race, has only two realistic contenders: Cork and Kerry. Indeed some commentators would suggest that Cork are still a bit behind the Kingdom.

A short few years ago the opposite was the case. Clare were always difficult opponents, especially in Ennis. Limerick under Liam Kerins came very close to winning the title in the last couple of years, and only a mighty leap by Dara Ó'Sé denied them that honour in 2004.

This season's championship was a mundane affair with the age-old rivals once again making it to the decider. However, en route they were less than impressive. Kerry stuttered and staggered past Waterford with a performance that outraged manager Jack O'Connor.

Tipperary were next up for the champions and while they never looked in trouble it was far from a convincing display by Kerry, even

if they did score 0-17. Worryingly, their most potent forward, Colm 'Gooch' Cooper, only managed one point and that from a free.

Cork and Limerick were in the other half of the draw. With another Kerry legend Mickey Ned O'Sullivan at the helm for the Shannonsiders, they quietly fancied their chances. Cork had just returned from a week of intensive training in La Manga, refreshed and ready for the challenge, or so they thought.

What transpired was without question the worst 70 minutes of championship football we were likely to witness all season. It was played before a paltry attendance in the Gaelic Grounds and on a pitch that resembled Banna Strand, it had so much sand on it. Not a pretty sight. And the football was just as bad.

The facts backs up this opinion. Limerick scored 4 points in the opening six minutes, added just one more in the remaining 29 minutes of the first half and failed to score in the second half. Cork's total was 0-9, with James Masters getting 0-8. It ended 0-9 to 0-5, a win for Billy Morgan's men.

There were few positives to be gleaned from an appalling match.

Except that Cork were in the Munster final and the Killarney publicans could look forward to a bonanza weekend, as the 'Rebel army' invaded 'Beauty's home'.

There was a strange atmosphere in Killarney on Sunday July 9th. Whether it was the fact that the World Cup final was on later that night or not, no one is quite sure. But the town in the hours preceding the game was relatively quiet. It was also felt that the Cork supporters, in light of the display in the semi final, just would not travel.

Kerry were also raging hot favourites, and the bookies rarely get it wrong.

However, what transpired was another epic encounter between these great rivals before a crowd of over 26,500, and, yes, this included a big Cork following. It had everything you could ask for in a Munster final, including a controversial finish.

It was Cork, with a team including seven Munster final debutants and altered at the throw-in to counter the Kerry danger men, that made the better start.

Kerry's Bryan Sheehan missed an easy free, against the breeze it must be said, before Cork took over. In nine minutes they hit three points. Kevin McMahon had one while James Masters added two.

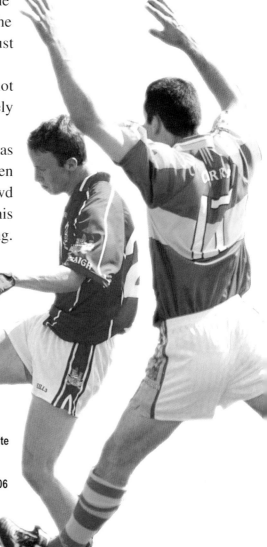

John Hayes, Cork, gets his kick away despite the attempted block by Tom O'Sullivan, Kerry. Cork v Kerry, Munster Football Final Replay, Páirc Uí Chaoimh, Cork. 16 July 2006

Colm Cooper, marked by Graham Canty, pointed a free which turned out to be his only score of the match, as the 'Gooch' continued to struggle with his form.

Cork remained in control. Their defence to a man was outstanding and easily contained the Kerry attack. Helped by the extraordinary work rate of those further out in the field, they denied Kerry time and space in which to launch attacks.

Kerry were struggling and could get little rhythm into their play. Jack O'Connor withdrew Mossie Lyons and brought on Tom O'Sullivan. Initially this change had little impact. Cork could have had a goal in the 21st minute but Donnacha O'Connor's great effort struck the butt of the upright, a real let-off for the champions.

Cork went further ahead as Masters, Fintan Goold and Kieran O'Connor all kicked points and it was now 0-7 to 0-1.

The 'Rebel' supporters were in full voice while the 'Kingdom' contingent were silenced by events unfolding before them. Kerry were on the ropes. Then just as quickly the direction of this intriguing contest turned.

A defining moment occurred in the 32nd minute. Cork's Anthony Lynch who had been involved in a running battle with Paul Galvin prior to this was the central character.

In a tussle for possession with Kieran Donaghy, he (Lynch) appeared to strike the Kerry midfielder with his elbow. Referee Joe McQuillan, after a brief consultation with his linesman, flashed a straight 'red card'. Lynch was off, Cork were down to 14 men.

Bryan Sheehan pointed the resultant free, which was Kerry's first score in 22 minutes. He quickly added two more before Declan O'Sullivan got his side's first point from play in first half injury time. So from a position of strength, Cork found their lead at the break whittled down to just three points at 0-7 to 0-4. With a strong wind to face in the second half, the initiative was firmly with Kerry.

Both sides made changes for the second half. Cork withdrew Donnacha O'Connor to accommodate an extra defender in

Lynch's absence. Kerry also withdrew an O'Connor debutant, in their case Paul O'Connor, and replaced him with Darren O'Sullivan.

O'Sullivan's pace troubled the Cork defence. He won an early free converted by Sheehan. The gap was now two points – 0-7 to 0-5. Cork were still in front.

A test of character for Billy Morgan's young team and they responded with two points from Masters whose free taking was exemplary. Cork had doubled their lead and their resolve.

However, Kerry had deployed Mike McCarthy as the extra man and slowly began to turn the screw. It was now Cork's turn to struggle.

Sheehan and Darren O'Sullivan both had points. Crucially it was to be another 12 minutes before Kerry scored again.

Cork were still working hard and limiting Kerry's opportunities, as first Cooper and then Sheehan missed easy frees that would have reduced the deficit further.

The extra man was now taking its toll on Cork, who to their credit were still battling hard, helped by the introduction of fresh legs in attack. Then came another major talking point when Kerry midfielder Kieran Donaghy was dismissed on a second yellow card. It was a harsh call on the young player.

It also gave Cork a lifeline and fresh impetus, as it broke Kerry's grip in midfield and Nicholas Murphy in particular thundered into the match.

Kerry weren't giving up yet though.

Paul Galvin kicked a point and after an Eoin Brosnan effort was deflected around the post Sheehan pointed the resultant '45' – level for the first time in the game. It was 0-9 to 0-9 and only ten minutes left.

The match was there to be won, and it appeared that Kerry had snatched it when Cooper's vision set up Sheehan who landed a massive point to put his side in front for the first time in the game.

Refusing to concede defeat, Cork battled back and good interplay between Kevin O'Sullivan and McMahon helped them win a free. Masters was coolness personified as he landed the levelling point on the 70th minute. Surely that was the last act of a draining contest and it was

James Masters, Cork, forces his way past Diarmuid Murphy, Kerry. Cork v Kerry, Munster Football Final Replay, Páirc Uí Chaoimh, Cork. 16 July 2006

all set for a replay in Cork a week later. But the drama was far from over.

Sensing the game was there for the taking and that Kerry were suddenly vulnerable, Cork came again. This time Kieran O'Connor, despite been enveloped in a sea of green and gold jerseys, managed to get a pass away to Masters. The angle was acute but his effort looked to have gone over the bar for the winning point. Amazing scenes followed. The

Cork supporters went wild with delight as the white flag was raised, but the umpire on the near side waved wide. Confusion reigned for a brief period. Kerry players surrounded the umpire who raised the flag. Referee McQuillan raced in and after a brief consultation with the men in white coats, the flags, green and white, were crossed to signify that the score would not stand. Still level 0-10 to 0-10 and despite a couple of more minutes of play, there was no further score.

The match had many talking points, especially the two dismissals. Both players would miss the replay on the banks of the Lee in Páirc Uí Chaoimh. Cork supporters were adamant the last effort was a point, but Masters admitted afterwards that it had gone wide.

Jack O'Connor was not happy with his side's display. He accepted that Cork had played very well and on that basis would be favourites for the replay.

Billy Morgan was delighted with how his young charges had handled the unique occasion that is a Munster final in Killarney. They would be a better team as a result, but it was still all to play for next Sunday.

If the town of Killarney was quiet before the game, it was positively buzzing afterwards as both sets of supporters discussed and digested the rights and wrongs of the afternoon's developments. Later on as the traffic snaked across the county bounds to Cork and back west to Tralee and Dingle, thoughts instantly turned to the next instalment of this age old and enduring rivalry. Berlin and the antics of one Zidane later in the evening were a million miles away, such is the appeal of a Cork and Kerry clash.

Munster Final

Kerry	**0-10**
Cork	**0-10**

The Final Countdown

July 16th, Páirc Uí Chaoimh: In the glorious summer sunshine, a determined Cork ran onto the pitch to face the Munster Football Champions in a much anticipated replay. The popular view was that Kerry would improve sufficiently to keep their title and prolong the wait for Cork's expected breakthrough. Cork received a huge boost 48 hours ahead of the game, when Anthony Lynch won an appeal against his sending-off in the previous match and was cleared to play. By contrast, Kerry were without influential midfielder Kieran Donaghy.

Kerry started purposefully and led by 0-3 to 0-1, but on 21 minutes Kieran O'Connor and John Hayes combined to set up James Masters for a wonderful goal to give Cork an important lead. The home side were in front at half-time by 1-4 to 0-5.

Cork were the fresher and fitter team and as the game entered its final quarter, a sense of anticipation surged through the crowd of 23,690. The majority were sporting red and white; there was a noticeable absence of green and gold.

Kerry tried manfully – none more so than Seamus Moynihan –

but the 'Gooch' and company in attack were well contained by the Cork defence. At the other end, a new scoring sensation etched his name into Munster final folklore.

James Masters finished with 1-6. He fired over a succession of quality points. Cork were champions on a 1-12 to 0-9 scoreline, and a 34th title was Leeside bound. It was a triumph for Cork manager Billy Morgan. Forty-three years after first appearing in a Munster final as a minor, he masterminded another victory over the 'old enemy'. The end of one era and perhaps the beginning of another one. Time alone will tell.

Munster Final Replay
Cork **1-12**
Kerry **0-9**

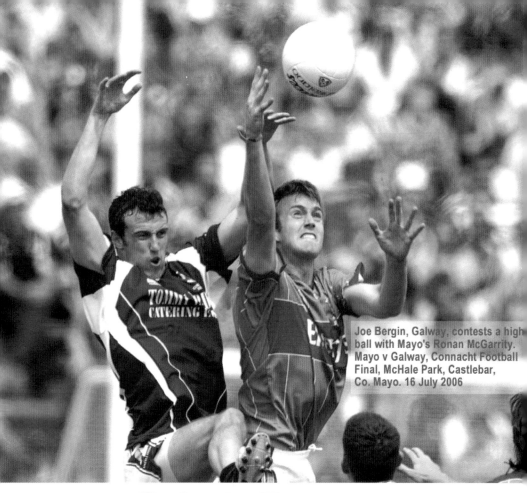

Joe Bergin, Galway, contests a high ball with Mayo's Ronan McGarrity. Mayo v Galway, Connacht Football Final, McHale Park, Castlebar, Co. Mayo. 16 July 2006

Old Rivals
IN CONNACHT

The Connacht Football Final was a close-scoring affair, in which two age-old rivals battled to be crowned the winner.

Galway v Mayo

Between them, Mayo and Galway have amassed a total of 84 Connacht titles. So it came as no real surprise that both teams qualified for the 2006 final in a provinc that, similar to Munster, produced poor fare fo the most part.

It was the second time in a matter of months that they clashed in McHale Park, Castlebar. Galway won a disappointing league semi final back in April, ending Mayo's interest in a competition that they had dominated for so long.

Significantly though, Mayo had replaced Galway as under-21 champions in the province and then went on to claim the All Ireland title with a win over Cork. Would this win inspire the seniors who for years have left their best form behind them?

The Championship is littered with Mayo failures. Their long-suffering supporters are to be commended for the unstinting support they continue to give their under-achieving senior team.

The build-up to the final had been as follows:

Roscommon and a large group of supporters made the trip to the 'Big Apple' for the first game of the 2006 Championship and there was a slight hint of a shock as New York, initially anyway, put up a good fight. In the end though, New York ran out of ideas and steam, and a collective sigh of relief could be heard on this side of the Atlantic.

Meanwhile, Mayo travelled to Ruislip and disposed of the challenge of London. In the first of the quarter finals, Galway got the better of Sligo to set up a semi final meeting with Roscommon.

Hyde Park was the venue and on a wet and windy day a strange contest evolved. Roscommon were in control and Galway could hardly buy a score. Then two quick goals completely deflated the home side and Peter Forde's men eased into yet another final.

Dermot Geraghty, Mayo, tries to deny possession to Michael Meehan, Galway. Mayo v Galway, Connacht Football Final, McHale Park, Castlebar, Co. Mayo. 16 July 2006

The tight and homely confines of Páirc MacDiarmuid in Carrick-on-Shannon was the venue for the clash of Leitrim and Mayo in the second semi final. Leitrim were brave and resilient but in the end a single point divided the sides. Mayo were back in the Connacht final with familiar opponents waiting in the wings.

With 34,613 supporters crammed into McHale Park, the hope was that the age-old rivals would deliver a game to remember.

Galway, despite the dominance of Mayo's Ronan McGarrity in midfield, held a narrow 0-5 to 0-4 lead at the break. However, Galway were dealt a blow on the stroke of half-time when star forward Sean Armstrong was forced off with an injury. With their attack misfiring as a unit, they could ill-afford to be without such an exciting player.

Mayo's defence was superb all through, but it was McGarrity who drove them on, even when others around him were struggling.

Galway moved Padraig Joyce into a two man full-forward line with Michael Meehan for the second half, but Joyce's creativity was missed further out the field. Despite their problems, Galway struck for a 44th minute goal. Damien Dunleavy's effort was half blocked, but Matthew Clancy reacted quickest to flick the ball into the net.

One minute later Joyce converted a free and Galway were now 1-7 to 0-6 ahead. In similar situations in the past Mayo teams would have folded, but manager Mickey Moran has instilled this group of players with tremendous self-belief. It surfaced as they battled back.

McGarrity was still dominating in midfield and at last his forwards took their cue from his inspirational play. In the space of five minutes they landed three points from Billy Joe Padden, Ger Brady and Alan Dillon. The gap was now just one point. Suddenly, the Mayo supporters sensed victory, even if they still trailed.

Cormac Bane and McGarrity traded points. Still the levelling score eluded Mayo. Then came a little cameo that ultimately turned the game, although at the time of happening very few realised it.

On 67 minutes played, Galway attacked and substitute Paul Clancy had possession. Declan

Conor Mortimer, Mayo, kicks the winning point in the final minutes of the Connacht Football Final, Mayo v Galway, McHale Park, Castlebar, Co. Mayo. 16 July 2006

Meehan was free but Clancy chose to shoot himself. His thundering drive struck the crossbar. A few minutes later at the other end, Mayo won a free, Kevin O'Neill converted it and the sides were level. It was a two point swing. In such a low scoring game, it was crucial.

It was now looking like a replay as the board signalled three minutes of added time, but there was to be one final twist.

Flashback first to the Connacht semi final of 2002 when Conor Mortimer missed a 20 metre 'gimme' of a free that cost Mayo dearly. Now Mortimer had the opportunity to banish that painful memory. The final whistle was merely a heartbeat away when Mayo were awarded a free. 'Dubious' was how one Galway mentor described it later. It was an acute angle and up stepped Mortimer. This time his effort dissected the posts. Mayo were in front and the clock was ticking into the third and final minute of injury time.

However, a slight delay allowed referee Paddy Russell to let the play continue. Galway worked the ball up the field and won a free about 37 metres from the posts. David Heaney was judged to have fouled Michael Donnellan.

The pressure was on Donnellan, Galway's favourite son, who in the past has worked near miraculous feats. Could he save his side? His radar though had been off all day and his dramatic effort fell left and short. Game over. And so for every hero, there's a villain. In this case Mortimer and Donnellan assume such roles.

Despite the closeness of the score, it was a disappointing decider. The last 10 minutes may have been absorbing but what went before will be quickly erased from the memory bank.

Both sides were guilty of poor play, 24 wides equally divided, misplaced passes and a litany of mistakes contrived to make it a final lacking in quality.

However, as hordes of green-and-red-clad supporters invaded the pitch, it was time for Mayo celebrations and can Mayo celebrate!

A proud captain David Heaney lifted the Nestor Cup and said what many supporters may have been thinking prior to the comeback,

'Maybe teams in the past would have withered but we didn't, we kept our composure and that stood to us in the end.'

For Galway boss Peter Forde, a Mayo man and resident in Castlebar, it was a huge disappointment. 'We failed to take our chances when on top, so now we must regroup for the qualifiers.'

So for Mayo, an under-21 and senior double in Connacht. Are they and their long-suffering supporters about to witness the ending of a famine that stretches back to 1951 (the last time Mayo won the Sam Maguire Cup) or will it be another false dawn? The coming weeks would provide the answer.

Connacht Final
Mayo 0-12
Galway 1-8

DJ CAREY
A HURLING LEGEND

There can't be too many people in Ireland who don't know that DJ Carey is a hurling legend. He announced his retirement this year, 2006, and a look back at his career undoubtedly proves exactly how great a legend he is!

It was Thursday, June 1st when Pat Treacy, a well-known journalist with the *Kilkenny Voice* newspaper, rang and advised me to 'check your email'.

I did and there it was. DJ Carey has announced his retirement from inter-county hurling. It may have been expected but when it finally came, it was still a shock. The departure of a great player, irrespective of the code, always is. It leaves a void that can at times be almost impossible to fill.

Kilkenny had just retained their league title and a few days beforehand, DJ lined out with his club Young Irelands in the county championship and scored 1-10. It appeared normal service had resumed.

A meeting with Kilkenny manager Brian Cody had been arranged for the previous Tuesday. Cody was confident that Carey would be part of his Championship plans, but the lad from Gowran had other ideas. The mind and spirit were willing but at 35 years of age, the body was saying otherwise. It was time to leave the stage at his own timing, and just as importantly, gracefully.

Another medal – be it Leinster or All Ireland – would make little difference to a reputation that had long been secured thanks to an honour-laden and brilliant career.

It was a career at inter-county level that spanned 16 years, bettered now by only one current player, Offaly's Brian Whelehan. It also yielded 43 goals and 195 points in 57 games, which by any standard is some record.

Ever since his days at that famous Kilkenny nursery, St Kieran's College, Denis Joseph Carey was destined for

the top. The first of his All Ireland medals was won in the 'black and white' hooped jerseys of the college. Grainy television or video footage was ample testimony that those watching were witnessing a star in the making. They were not disappointed.

Hurling was always his first love, but DJ was an outstanding handballer and won several All Ireland titles at various grades.

DJ also played football with his club.

Indeed he picked up an injury in one game which caused him to miss a few hurling matches. In a county where the 'big ball' game is very much an afterthought, this did not sit well with some people. However, Carey was his own man and he saw it as his duty to play with his club.

In all his years playing he was never once sent off nor even had his name taken. Yellow or red cards were never flashed in his direction – that in itself is a remarkable record and one of which he is justifiably proud.

The timing of his departure may have been a surprise, but it was the right thing to do as he explains. 'Well, I feel the time is right. I am 35 years of age and I'm not prepared to put my body through the rigours of another championship campaign, especially now that Brian (Cody), has developed a nice new team that is well capable of winning this year's All Ireland title.'

He continued 'I will carry on playing with Young Irelands which I am really enjoying and without the pressure of inter-county hurling can give something back to my club that has stood by me in good and bad times; at least I owe them that much.'

DJ also felt it would have been wrong to go after the semi final loss to Galway last year (2005). 'I wanted to play the club games to see if the serious drive was there but it wasn't. I'm busy work-wise and with a lot of other stuff. I've been playing ok with the club and enjoying it but I wouldn't have the real appetite to commit to going back with Kilkenny. That's a totally different pace.'

Tributes to his talent dominated air time once the news broke and all of these have been fulsome in their praise of one of the game's greatest hurlers. DJ was in many respects the GAA's first gilt-edged superstar, as he played the game in a media-driven era, far different from those who had gone before him. Ring, Mackey and

DJ Carey, Kilkenny v Tipperary,
Allianz National Hurling League,
Nowlan Park, Kilkenny. 24 April 2005

Rackard did not have to contend with the countless previews and reviews, quotes and misquotes. They played the game almost without intrusion.

Of course, DJ himself was ever the gentlemen when it came to interviews. He was always available to answer a call or give a quote.

In 1998, he first contemplated retirement and actually stepped off the stage for a brief period – six weeks in fact. However, after receiving 25,000 letters, he had a change of heart and quickly returned to the game he loved. A further setback came in 2002 when he was involved in a car crash and the injuries sustained clearly hampered him for some time. Yet later that year he was part of a Kilkenny team that collected the Liam McCarthy Cup and one year later the ultimate accolade of another medal as Kilkenny captain.

Hurling will be the poorer without him. He had a true genius and relied on talent, creativity and a willingness to try new things. His was a household name, even to those who only had a passing interest in the game.

He was the first hurler to hire an agent, Barbara Galavan who spent 17 years working with U2. The video of his career is the bestselling sports video of all time in Ireland. Golf is another great passion of his. Now that the camán has been put away, the man who is on first name terms with Tiger Woods will enjoy a few leisurely rounds without the pressure of inter-county training.

Another aspect of his life that is rarely mentioned is his work for the charity GOAL. DJ has journeyed to the most poverty-stricken corners of the world to raise awareness of the plight of young children in an effort to bring some joy and happiness into a life that few of us care to acknowledge actually exists. Many charities and clubs have benefited from DJ's presence at some function or other and as many an official will tell you, money was never an issue.

One particularly difficult period for DJ came in the lead-up to the 2003 All Ireland final. At the time he had just separated from his wife Christine. Several newspapers actually stalked him in the build-up to the game, and it prompted Eamonn Dunphy and Liam Griffin to appeal on

DJ Carey, in action for Kilkenny. 10 September 2000

television to one particular newspaper not to delve into his private life on match day.

DJ was bemused by it all: 'I found it mind boggling that a multi billion-dollar corporation were going after a small fry from rural Ireland just because he has a profile in amateur sport.'

Some papers ran with the story, others skirted around the issue, but he received unstinting support from his colleagues on the Kilkenny team and especially from manager Brian Cody.

In advance of the match, Cody approached him and assured him of their full backing. DJ went on to win his fifth All Ireland medal a few days later. It was the perfect response.

These are just side issues. DJ was first and foremost a hurler and one of rare talent. Those of us who enjoy the game should remember him for his feats on the field.

Born in Gowran in 1970, he has three brothers and three sisters, one of whom, Catriona, is an international hockey player. His family are steeped in the game. His aunt Peggy won four All Ireland medals in camogie. His grand-uncle Paddy Phelan was an iconic hurler in the 1930s and was selected on the team of the century and also on the An Post team of the Millennium.

That DJ missed out on that accolade still baffles people.

There are those, of course, who will point to some flaws in DJ's game. He played in nine All Ireland finals and failed to score in four of them. In two other finals, his tally was only one point from play. In his four finals against Cork, he managed just two points. Thus the comment that he failed to deliver on the big occasions. The facts suggest otherwise.

In 2000 against Offaly he bagged 1-4, while two years later against Clare that increased to 1-6, including a superb point from the sideline, without playing the ball from his hand. A touch of genius. To dwell on such matters is only nitpicking. His legacy is safe and as he said himself, 'it is not always about scores, there is so much more to hurling.' Hooking, blocking, passing and creating scores for those around him were attributes he had in abundance.

One of his best displays came in the 1997 All Ireland quarter final. Kilkenny trailed Galway by nine points. DJ inspired a fightback, scored 2-7 and the 'Cats' won.

The tributes following the announcement of his retirement poured in. Wexford's Liam Dunne acknowledged his 'bravery', Brian Whelehan called him the 'greatest Kilkenny hurler ever', Johnny Dooley described him as the 'best of his generation'.

Former Kilkenny great Eddie Keher's comment that 'he is the most complete hurler I have ever seen as he mastered every skill in the game' is fitting tribute to a master craftsman.

Current manager Brian Cody paid him due tribute by saying his influence in the dressing room was very important. 'The younger players would have watched DJ win his early medals and loved him, but they quickly found out he was the most accommodating and most encouraging superstar they ever met and he helped in the development of every single youngster on our team.'

All major honours in the game came his way. It makes impressive reading – five All Ireland senior medals, eight Leinster Championships, four National Leagues, Hurler of the Year in 1993 and 2000, three Railway Cups with Leinster, two County Championship medals and a record-equalling (with Pat Spillane) nine All-Star awards. In handball he won a total of 22 All Ireland medals as well as two All Ireland titles. In football, he won an Intermediate county medal and a similar honour in hurling.

It's time now though to move on to another phase in his life, a life that he shares with his partner Sarah Newman in their residence in Monkstown, County Dublin.

It will be a life without inter-county hurling, hard to imagine, but he leaves with his place secure in the annals of the GAA.

As a famous politician stated on his retirement, 'I have done the state some service, they know that'. DJ did the GAA some service, they know that. Don't they just.

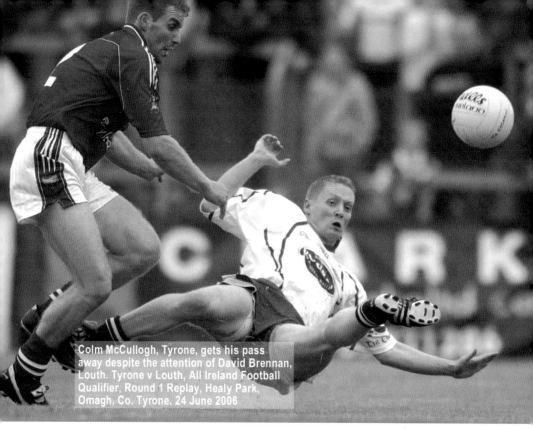

Colm McCullogh, Tyrone, gets his pass away despite the attention of David Brennan, Louth. Tyrone v Louth, All Ireland Football Qualifier, Round 1 Replay, Healy Park, Omagh, Co. Tyrone. 24 June 2006

FOOTBALL QUALIFIERS
DELIVER DRAMA
Rounds 1 and 2

And so the qualifiers begin. Faced with the threat of elimination from the Championship, each team fights to stay in the competition. Some shocks were in store, however . . .

Round 1					
Tyrone	v	Louth	Sligo	v	Down
Monaghan	v	Wicklow	Waterford	v	Longford
Westmeath	v	London	Carlow	v	Meath
Antrim	v	Clare	Kildare	v	Cavan

Saturday, June 17th Páirc Tailteann in Navan. This could well be described as the evening the Bank of Ireland Football Championship sprung into life. Before this game the respective provincial championships had offered little. The only real surprise was Tyrone's defeat to Derry. They also suffered the ignominy of failing to score in the first half. Now an improving Louth were waiting in the wings.

Tyrone were hit with a catalogue of injuries in advance of this match and also during it. Key players, including Stephen O'Neill, were forced out of the action.

The All Ireland champions produced some sparkling play in the first half. With Owen Mulligan at the hub of everything, they were 2-7 to 0-5 in front at the break. Mulligan helped himself to 2-3.

The 'Wee County' were a different team in the second half. They scored three early points and when Mark Stanfield blasted the ball to the net, it was game on again: 2-7 to 1-8. Louth carried the fight to Tyrone and with Darren Clarke unerring with his free taking, there was just three points between the sides as the clock edged towards the 70 minute mark.

One last raid by Louth produced the equalising goal, fisted to the net by JP Rooney to force extra-time. Louth actually took the lead during that 20-minute period and

Tyrone were facing elimination from the Championship. However, champions die hard and in a nail-biting finish, Owen Mulligan pointed two frees to send the sides to Healy Park, Omagh for a replay a week later. Fittingly, both teams were given a standing ovation by the 7,000 plus crowd as the Championship finally came alive.

The replay went the way of the champions who on this occasion did not allow a big lead slip. It was 1-10 to 0-3 at half-time. Louth did mount a spirited comeback as Tyrone were reduced to 14 men, but there was to be no shock in Omagh. Tyrone ran out winners by 1-12 to 1-7. Their season was back on track. Worryingly for Mickey Harte, the injuries continued to mount up.

Elsewhere, results were along predictable lines, although Down's meagre tally of just 0-4 in their loss to Sligo was a major blow to a proud football county.

Clare were annoyed at having to travel to Belfast for their game with Antrim on Saturday afternoon. They chartered a plane at a reputed cost of €20,000, but left for Shannon, happy at their 1-13 to 2-9 win.

Longford, having tested Dublin in the Leinster Championship before a full house in Pearse Park, now found themselves playing in a near deserted Walsh Park. However, they still recorded a 1-16 to 1-9 win over Waterford. Westmeath had an easy win over London.

Monaghan got the better of Wicklow by 2-19 to 3-6, while in another intriguing encounter Carlow were paired against Meath. Carlow manager Liam Hayes was facing a county he had represented with distinction during his playing career.

In advance of the game, Hayes annoyed many in the Royal County with some of his comments, but it was the men from Meath who did the talking on the pitch. Carlow were competitive, but Meath were smarter and more clinical. They ran out winners by 1-17 to 0-12.

The one remaining game in this round was delayed a week owing to the 'Blood Sub' controversy in Leinster. Kildare put it behind them, and in the process ended Cavan's Championship season with a comfortable win 0-18 to 1-7 before an 8,000 crowd in Newbridge.

Round 2

Tyrone	v	Laois	Wexford	v	Monaghan
Derry	v	Kildare	Sligo	v	Leitrim
Longford	v	Tipperary	Fermanagh	v	Clare
Meath	v	Roscommon	Westmeath	v	Limerick

Tyrone desperately wanted to retain their All Ireland title, but they were certainly going about it the hard way. Having needed extra-time and a replay to see off Louth, next up were Mick O'Dwyer's Laois.

Laois were badly stung by the manner in which Dublin had beaten them. Micko, now in his last year with the county, took immediate action. In a throwback to his Kerry days, he adopted a hands-on approach to training in advance of this critical encounter. The Waterville maestro was determined that his legacy to his adopted county would not be the debacle he had witnessed in Croke Park.

Tyrone were vulnerable and the conditions did not suit them. Driving wind and rain enveloped O'Moore Park in Portlaoise – all the ingredients for a surprise result.

Laois had the elements at their backs for the first half but only led by 0-6 to 0-3 at the break. Would it be enough given the strength of the wind?

The home side were superb in the second half as they continually worked the ball the length of the field with neat intricate passing. The longer it went on, the more you sensed Tyrone's exit was imminent.

Laois went ahead by four points early in the second half. With the much-heralded Tyrone attack starved of possession, scores were scarce. In fact, in the second half it took the champions 15 minutes to register a score with the wind. Tyrone

did cut the lead to two points with the sands of time running out. Chris Conway stretched it to three in the final minutes. Laois looked safe. Tyrone needed a goal to save their crown. It never looked like coming and it never did. The champions were out and Mick O'Dwyer at 70 years of age masterminded another famous win.

Johnny McBride, Derry, in action against John Doyle, Kildare. All Ireland Senior Football Qualifier, Round 2, Derry v Kildare, Celtic Park, Derry. 1 July 2006

The crowd of over 9,500 forgot the dismal weather and savoured the occasion.

However, amidst it all there was a tinge of sympathy for the fallen champions.

Mickey Harte was gracious as ever, even in defeat. He vowed that Tyrone would be back.

Derry also signalled their intent with a thumping victory over Kildare at Celtic Park. The Oak Leaf County are making a habit of winning games in the qualifiers.

Paddy Bradley was once again in fine form as they played with a flair and freedom that was sadly lacking in their loss to Donegal in the Ulster championship.

Bradley notched up six points as he teased and tormented an outclassed Kildare defence. Johnny McBride grabbed the goal in a 1-17 to 0-10 win that was signposted from very early on.

Luke Dempsey's Longford ran Tipperary ragged on their home patch. With David Barden getting an early goal there was never much doubt about the outcome. It eventually ended 1-23 to 1-10.

There was a big win for under-pressure Meath boss Eamonn Barry and his team against Roscommon. It prompted Roscommon manager John Maughan to say after the game, 'I wish the referee could have stopped it early in the second half'. It is easy to see why as Meath won by 1-19 to 0-9.

There was an exciting contest in Cusack Park, Mullingar as Westmeath staged a fabulous comeback to end Limerick's season. The Shannonsiders raced into an early lead of 1-5 to 0-1, helped by Micheal Reidy's goal, but by half-time the gap was a manageable 1-6 to 0-6.

Westmeath were hampered by the dismissal of James Davitt with 15 minutes remaining. However, having drawn level with Donal O'Donoghue's 70th minute free, they snatched victory with an injury time winner from Michael Ennis.

Wexford and Mattie Forde put the events of the previous week, on and off the pitch, behind them to record a commendable win over Monaghan in Clones. Forde once again demonstrated his value to the team by scoring six points in a narrow 0-8 to 0-6 win.

In an all-Connacht clash, Leitrim, for the second game in a row, were at the wrong end of a one point defeat. This time Sligo

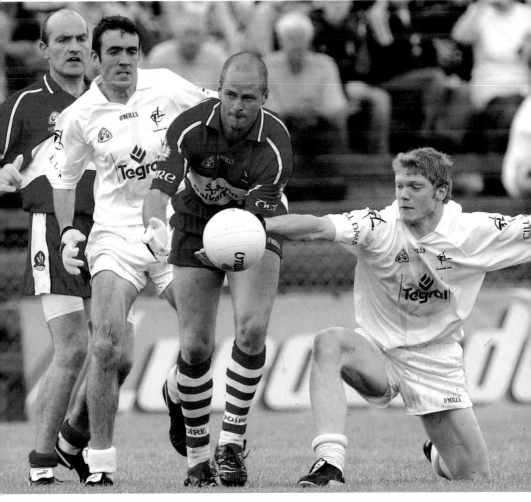

Kevin McCloy, Derry, manages to evade Tomas Connor, Kildare. Derry v Kildare, All Ireland Football Qualifier, Round 2, Celtic Park, Derry. 1 July 2006

prevailed by 0-10 to 1-6.

Fermanagh, who had an excellent record in the qualifiers, maintained their good run with a 0-15 to 0-10 win over Clare in Ennis.

Just one more round of qualifiers to be played before the beaten provincial finalists would join the battle for a place in the last eight. It was now getting very interesting and after the result from Portlaoise, a new name, or maybe an old one, would be inscribed on the base of the cup come September.

Colin Lynch, Clare, tries to hold on to the ball with Barry Foley, Limerick, trying to dispossess him. Clare v Limerick, All Ireland Hurling Qualifier, Round 1, Cusack Park, Ennis, Co. Clare. 18 June 2006

THE (FADING) APPEAL OF THE HURLING QUALIFIERS

Is it time for a major re-think of the hurling qualifiers?

Section A
Galway, Waterford, Laois, Westmeath
Section B
Clare, Limerick, Offaly, Dublin

Wexford's victory over Offaly in a dour and disappointing Guinness Leinster Hurling semi final cleared the way for the draw for the qualifiers, now in their second and possibly final year.

A special Congress will determine the format

for the 2007 season. It is the opinion of many that the qualifiers are of little value given that there is an air of inevitability about the outcome even before they commence.

It was also the view that the respective Munster and Leinster champions should receive some reward for winning their provincial titles. As it currently stands, a team could lose twice, yet end up at the same stage of the Championship as Cork and Kilkenny. Limerick's performance this year is an example of this phenomenon. Cork boss John Allen and his Kilkenny counterpart Brian Cody said such a situation diminishes the provincial championships.

Having already reached the Munster final, both Cork and Tipperary had ensured they would not have to endure the 'pool stages' of a Championship that was rapidly losing its appeal.

Kilkenny, by virtue of their easy win over Westmeath, also avoided the trawl around the country. They could look forward, along with their old rivals Wexford, to a quarter final place in late July.

Eight teams then entered the 'drum' for the group stages. In Clones after the Ulster Football semi final, GAA President Nickey Brennan, Rory Sheridan of sponsors Guinness and RTÉ's Marty Morrissey presided over the draw.

Certain permutations were not allowed but in his own inimitable style Marty explained it with ease and everything went like clockwork.

So after the 'roll of the drum' the following sections emerged to begin the race for a place in the last eight of the All Ireland Hurling Championship.

Section A contained Galway, Waterford, Laois and Westmeath.

Section B contained Clare, Limerick, Offaly and Dublin.

The first round games were scheduled for the weekend of June 17th/18th. Even before a ball was pucked, some counties were given little chance of progressing.

It should also be pointed out that three counties because of their standing were given 'designated county status' which ensured they would get two home games.

Dublin, Westmeath and Laois were the teams nominated, but would that improve their chances of making progress? Unlikely.

First Round

Of the four games scheduled, only one proved competitive. The big clash of **Clare** and **Limerick** had its own drama, both at half-time and full time.

Offaly just got the better of tenacious **Dublin** in an exciting contest in Parnell Park before a crowd of 7,000, where the influence of Offaly's Brian Whelehan was a crucial factor.

Dublin in their first outing since losing to Westmeath in the Portlaoise pond gave an excellent display and could face the remaining rounds with restored confidence.

The sides were level five times before Whelehan's goal in the 32nd minute gave Offaly a lead they never relinquished. Despite strong Dublin pressure, they held on to win by 1-17 to 0-17.

It was all one way traffic in Portlaoise as **Galway** took their Championship bow and handed out a lesson to **Laois**. It was done and dusted at half-time as Conor Hayes' men led 3-8 to 0-6.

The Galway full-forward line plundered 7-5 from play as they eventually racked up 7-18, while the Laois tally of 2-13 was creditable enough in the circumstances.

Westmeath enjoyed home advantage for their game with **Waterford**. To their credit, they kept the score respectable, but there was never a hint of a shock.

It was 2-14 to 0-6 at the break and while Waterford eased up somewhat in the second half, they still had too much in hand and were comfortable winners 3-22 to 1-14 at the finish.

Much was expected for the all-Munster clash of neighbours Clare and Limerick before a large crowd in Cusack Park, Ennis.

Both sides had a lot to play for after disappointing exits from the provincial championship. However, only one team left with pride intact, the other left with morale shattered.

The scoreboard never lies: Clare 2-21 Limerick 0-10.

In fact, Limerick only scored one point from play as Clare hit 11 without reply in a 14-minute spell.

All was clearly not well in the Limerick camp. Rumours were rife of dressing room unrest at half-time, confirmed by the resignation of Manager Joe McKenna and selector Ger Cunningham within two hours of the end of the match.

Limerick manager Joe McKenna, left, Dave Mahedy, trainer, centre, and Ger Cunningham, selector. Clare v Limerick, All Ireland Hurling Qualifier, Round 1, Cusack Park, Ennis, Co. Clare. 18 June 2006

The shortest journey Limerick have to undertake in hurling is to Ennis. The return trip that night was surely the longest. Once again, Limerick hurling was in crisis.

Two days after this hammering the Limerick County Board put a new management team in place. Former stars Ritchie Bennis and Gary Kirby joined selector Liam Lenihan in what could best be described now as a 'salvage operation'.

Second Round

All eyes were on O'Connor Park, Tullamore as the new Limerick management dipped their toes in the Championship water for the very first time on 1st July, 2006. To the credit of the players they responded in style. **Offaly** were simply blown away and a much changed **Limerick** amassed an impressive tally of 2-29 in a comfortable win even if they did trail at one stage. Offaly themselves scored 2-19, good enough to win most matches but not on this occasion. It was a real hammer blow to Offaly's ambitions.

Clare, as expected, had an easy win over **Dublin** (4-21 to 1-16), ensuring Anthony Daly's men would head the group entering the final series of matches.

It meant that with a very good scoring return, Clare were almost certainly assured of securing the top spot and thus avoiding a meeting with either Cork or Kilkenny in the last eight.

Offaly and Limerick had two points each and with Clare and Dublin respectively to play in the last round, the odds favoured Limerick reaching the quarter finals at Offaly's expense. In the light of events in Ennis a few short weeks earlier, that would constitute a major achievement for the

new look Limerick team. Dublin for all their early season promise had little to show for their efforts.

The big game in Section A between **Waterford** and **Galway** would decide the top spot. And what a scoring spectacle it produced before more than 11,000 spectators in Walsh Park! Waterford with home advantage and boosted by the return of Eoin Kelly and a fully fit John Mullane played some great hurling.

Galway matched them in most areas but a crucial double switch on 20 minutes by Justin McCarthy swung the game in

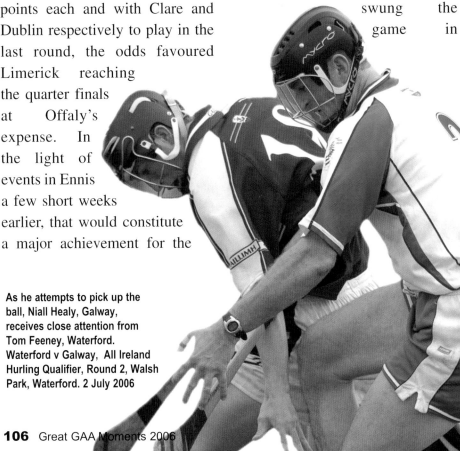

As he attempts to pick up the ball, Niall Healy, Galway, receives close attention from Tom Feeney, Waterford. Waterford v Galway, All Ireland Hurling Qualifier, Round 2, Walsh Park, Waterford. 2 July 2006

Waterford's direction.

It was an ultra competitive tie right from the start. It had all the necessary ingredients – quality play, fabulous scores and for good measure a sending-off (Galway's David Collins on 50 minutes). The vital goal arrived five minutes later courtesy of a Paul Flynn free and from there to the finish, Waterford held the upper hand.

Galway did pinch two goals but the home side had done enough to earn a deserved victory and with it a place in the last eight of the Championship as group winners.

Laois recorded a narrow 2-10 to 1-9 win over **Westmeath**, giving beleaguered manager Dinny Cahill a first Championship win.

So with one series of games still to be played it seemed likely that Galway, Waterford, Clare and Limerick would claim the four spots on offer.

Exactly as everyone predicted when the draw was made!

Third Round

So to the third and final round.

It was a wet and dank evening in Ennis as **Offaly** trailed **Clare** when Brian Whelehan entered the fray twenty minutes from time.

However, there were no heroics from the only modern-day hurler to make the 'millennium team', and despite his best efforts, the Faithful County departed the Championship.

Supporters probably saw the great Brian Whelehan in action for the very last time. In truth, Offaly never really recovered from their loss to Wexford in the Leinster semi final and they were on a downward spiral since. For the second season in a row, they failed to make it out of the qualifiers.

Limerick completed their rehabilitation by defeating **Dublin** to join Clare in the quarter final draw.

In Group A, Dinny Cahill's **Laois** season ended where it all began – on a wet and windy day in O'Moore Park, Portlaoise – as **Waterford** confirmed their place as group winners.

Galway dished out another heavy beating to luckless **Westmeath** and the minnows in this group series must ask themselves was it all worth it.

So after a three game series that took the best part of a month to complete, there were no shocks or no surprises and more to the point very few, if any, games of consequence.

Crowds at most games were small, Galway and Waterford the exception, and a major rethink is needed as clearly the present format is not working.

Once again it was over to Marty Morrissey in a now deserted Croke Park, along with Nickey Brennan and Rory Sheridan of Guinness, to preside over the quarter final draw.

This is what everyone was waiting for, this is where the real race for honours would begin. No more back doors or safety nets. It was winner takes all from here on in. The following pairings emerged: Cork v Limerick, Kilkenny v Galway, Clare v Wexford and Tipperary v Waterford. All these games were fixed for the weekend of July 22nd/23rd where it was the fervent hope of all hurling supporters that the season would finally come to life.

Donegal manager Brian McIver, left, and Armagh manager Joe Kernan at a photocall on the weekend of the Bank of Ireland Ulster Football Final. Bank of Ireland Head Office, Baggot Street, Dublin. 4 July 2006

ULSTER FOOTBALL FINAL
Ulster Heads South

Armagh v Donegal

Donegal and Armagh take their battle to be the Ulster Football Final winners to Croke Park.

St Tiernach's Park in Clones, County Monaghan has long been the spiritual home of the Ulster Football Final. The huge bank directly opposite the main stand is an imposing sight and it has witnessed many an epic decider.

Clones town and its business people were beneficiaries over a long period as crowds flocked to the venue for the biggest football day in the province.

Time was of course when the winning of an Ulster title satisfied most counties, Down being the notable exception. Down was the first county to bring the Sam Maguire Cup across the border. Kerry and Dublin were the dominant teams and everyone else sat back and admired the big two.

Donegal were the first, after Down, to break the mould by winning the All Ireland in 1992. Derry, Armagh and Tyrone have since followed and suddenly Ulster football is fashionable again. It is now the most competitive of the provincial championships as in any given year six or seven counties are capable of winning it.

This has ensured a higher profile for the championship and with a higher profile comes bigger crowds and for bigger crowds you need bigger and better stadiums. So three years ago the Ulster Council took the decision, and a brave one it was, to move their football final to Croke Park. It's a decision that is reviewed on a yearly basis.

It must be said that St Tiernach's Park is now a fine stadium. Its capacity is 36,000. The Ulster Council are to be commended for the development work that they have undertaken in recent years. However, with the growth of the championship it just could not cater for the huge volume of support that teams such as Tyrone, Armagh and Donegal now enjoy.

Initially there was a huge outcry from the business people of Clones. Many said they were dependent on the Ulster Final to see them through the year. However, the Ulster Council's first duty is to their counties and in truth they owed the Clones business people nothing. Having played their finals there for a long number of years, they had more than contributed to the economic well-being of the town.

The 2004 final between Armagh and Donegal was the first to be played outside of the province, Armagh's draw and replay with Tyrone followed last year. For the third successive season, the Orchard County is involved, with Donegal providing the opposition. In each case the Council's decision was vindicated with in excess of 50,000 supporters attending the deciders.

This year's draw kept the big wo – Armagh and Tyrone – on opposite sides. Given their espective strengths they were on course for a collision in the final. But in keeping with the trend of he championship in recent years, here was a surprise or two along he way.

Early rounds went to form. Down got the better of Cavan and Fermanagh, as expected, beat Antrim. Then came the result that ent shock waves through the province and beyond.

Derry not only beat Tyrone but he champions ailed to score in he first half. The qualifiers beckoned or Mickey Harte's nen.

Donegal got the etter of Down in a cracker at Ballybofey and ollowed that with a win over Derry to make it o the final, despite a few nternal squabbles along the way.

Armagh were now favourites to retain the title, but were making hard work of reaching the final. Monaghan held Joe Kernan's men to a draw in their first game before they won the replay. They were then decidedly lucky to scramble a draw with Fermanagh before making no mistake at the second time of asking. Would these extra matches take their toll on what some viewed as an ageing Armagh squad?

Malachy Macklin, Armagh, is determined to get past the challenge of Neil McGee, Donegal. Donegal v Armagh, Ulster Football Final, Croke Park, Dublin. 9 July 2006

All would be revealed in Croke Park on July 9th as once again Ulster heads South. Less than 24 hours before the game, the championship took on a new dimension as All Ireland champions Tyrone made their exit at the hands of Laois in the qualifiers. From Armagh's point of view, this was a major obstacle removed.

So Armagh were favourites as they sought their sixth Ulster title in eight years, as well as a three-in-a-row, last achieved by the great Down team of the '60's. But this was an Armagh with three 30-somethings in their side. Could they once again create their own piece of history? In fact all three players were awesome. One of them, Francie Bellew, was named man of the match. Not bad for a man who was once the butt of Pat Spillane's jokes about his grandmother's likely ability to outrun the Armagh player.

Donegal were dealt a blow in the build-up to the game when their free taker, Michael Doherty, was ruled out with injury. Armagh were quickest out of the blocks, but as the game progressed it soon became clear that scores would be at a premium and defences would dominate.

Oisin McConville's sixth minute free took his tally in the Ulster championship one ahead of the great Peter Canavan as the highest scorer in the province. Ronan Clarke kicked two Armagh points, but one by Barry Dunnion for Donegal was the pick of the first half scores. It came at the end of a six-man move that ripped Armagh apart. All to play for at half-time, sides level at 0-4 apiece.

Referee Michael Monahan was not helping matters. It was by no means a dirty game, tough and typical Ulster really. However, 13 yellow cards were issued over the 70 minutes, some of them for the most trivial of offences.

The crowd were hoping that the second half would finally ignite, but the opposite happened. Maybe it was the timing of the game's only goal.

It arrived in the first minute of the second half, a beauty by Paul McGrane. From here on the intensity seemed to drain out of the occasion. The expected Donegal response failed to materialise. The game lacked the drama and passion normally associated with Ulster championship matches. For the next 25 minutes, without ever having to do much, Armagh set the tone of the contest. They could even afford the luxury, if such is the case, of having goals by Steven McDonnell and Ronan Clarke disallowed.

Donegal manager Brian McIver emptied the bench in an effort to retrieve his side's flagging hopes of taking the Anglo-Celt Cup back to Tír Conail. But this Armagh side was not for turning, yet only McGrane's quality goal divided the sides.

It was only with the sands of time running out and the PA system instructing stewards to assume their end-of-match positions that Donegal discovered a sense of urgency.

But the wily old heads in the champion's side surfaced and they used it to good effect in the closing stages, especially Kieran McGeeney.

McGeeney has been the heartbeat of this team since they emerged as a force on the national stage. Now operating in midfield, he gave a masterful display, niggling away at the opposition whether they had possession or not and also covering acres of ground. However, he reserved his

Neil Gallagher, Donegal, rises highest to win possession from his team-mate Paddy Campbell and Armagh's Paul McGrane. Donegal v Armagh, Ulster Football Final, Croke Park, Dublin. 9 July 2006

best move until this contest was heading for its finality.

Donegal were pressing hard, Eamonn McGee was about to pull the trigger for what would have been the equalising goal, when McGeeney got in to bat the ball to safety. It was the last chance to force a replay. Armagh were not to be denied, Ulster champions again by 1-9 to 0-9.

The stewards were powerless to prevent the invasion of Orchard County fans onto the pitch and the presentation area, a familiar sight as the Cup was handed over. Watching the proceedings was one Paul Caffrey, the Dublin manager, in his capacity as a Garda on duty, no doubt thinking ahead to his own team's day of destiny a week later.

Joe Kernan was thrilled 'to win six championships in eight years is a wonderful achievement and we had to work very hard for each of them, but this is a very special group of players who take great pride in wearing the Armagh jersey, and deserve all the plaudits that come their way'.

However, sweet as it is, you sense that the Anglo-Celt Cup will be quietly stored away for the time being. Armagh have their eyes on a bigger cup. Sam Maguire has eluded this team since its one and only visit to the county in 2002. It is the only Cup they want to parade around the county.

Tyrone are gone, Kerry are still not out of Munster. Are Armagh finally going to scratch that itch and claim a second All Ireland title?

Kernan again, 'We have been at this stage for the last three years and we haven't done it, we are where we want to be, but a lot of things can happen between now and September.'

How right he is in that assessment, but for now yet another Ulster championship is at an end. As the supporters travelled back across the border, it's Armagh who are once again celebrating on an afternoon when an Ulster invasion of the capital city resembled a stroll in the July sunshine.

Dublin supporters on Hill 16.
Dublin v Offaly, Leinster Football Final,
Croke Park, Dublin. 16 July 2006

LEINSTER FOOTBALL FINAL
THE DUBS MARCH ON

Dublin v Offaly

The Leinster Football Championship provided surprises and some great football, culminating in an exciting and packed final in Croke Park.

Ever since their re-emergence as a major force under Kevin Heffernan in 1974, the 'Dubs' have commanded huge support, be it at home or away. This trend was maintained as the Bank of Ireland Leinster Football Championship of 2006 got underway.

In the opening round they were paired with Longford, a repeat of their 2005 clash which

Dublin won in a canter. The Leinster Council decided that on this occasion Longford would have home advantage. This would result in a substantial financial loss as Pearse Park can only hold 15,000 whereas if it was played in Croke Park in excess of 50,000 would have attended.

There was intense pressure on the Council to switch the game to accommodate the huge Dublin support. They resisted all overtures and the game went ahead as planned.

The Longford county board put in a huge effort and on the day they got their reward. The sun shone and the revamped stadium looked resplendent as the Dublin bandwagon rolled into town.

On the field, Longford under the guidance of experienced Luke Dempsey really tested the 'Dubs'. Later in the season they would prove it was not just a one-off, but Dublin, although far from impressive, did enough to win and secure a place in the semi final.

In the other first round games there was little to get excited about. Offaly, Westmeath, Carlow and Meath had their expected wins, but the first shock would soon arrive.

Wexford, although relegated to Division 2 of the league, outsmarted Eamonn Barry's Meath in the quarter final, heaping more pressure on the beleaguered manager who has endured a torrid time since taking over from Sean Boylan.

Kildare and Offaly had a lively hour but the match, which Offaly won, was overshadowed by the 'Blood Sub' controversy which dragged on for the best part of three weeks.

Laois, meanwhile, in Mick O'Dwyer's last year in charge, set up a semi final meeting with Dublin that would attract over 60,000 to Croke Park. If Dublin struggled in their win over Longford, well they were positively brilliant in dismissing the O'Moore County with a clinical display. It was so good that the odds on the 'Dubs' winning their first All Ireland title since 1995 were drastically cut.

Offaly and Wexford was the pairing for the second semi final and the match was notable for an incident involving Mattie Forde, Wexford's top player. Offaly won an excellent game to march on to a final meeting with their old foes Dublin, rekindling memories of some fascinating battles in the not too distant past.

However, the incident with Forde, in which he appeared to stamp on the head of Offaly player Shane O'Sullivan, dominated the headlines. To compound matters, the incident was shown on the big screen in the stadium and it certainly did not reflect much credit on Forde. Referee Jimmy White who did not see the incident took no action. Forde and Wexford had an anxious few days' wait before knowing if and how he was to be punished.

That aside, the stage was set for an epic Leinster Final that was sure to have the full house signs up in Croke Park, a regular occurrence when Dublin are playing.

In contrast with the Leinster Hurling Final, which was a mundane and dull affair played before a muted and uninterested crowd, this was special. Croke Park was packed with 81,754. The atmosphere was electric and as the teams entered the arena, they were greeted by a kaleidoscope of colour and a

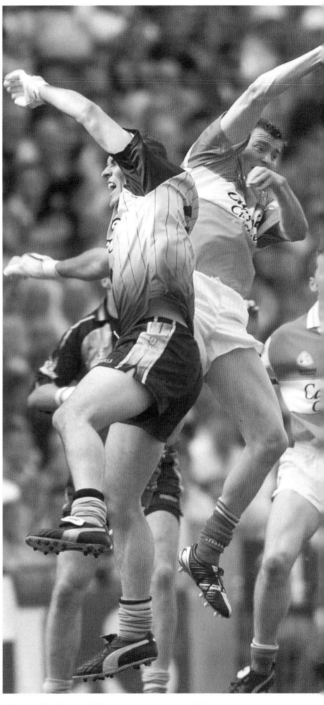

Ciaran Whelan, Dublin, in action against Ciaran McManus, Offaly. Dublin v Offaly, Leinster Football Final, Croke Park, Dublin. 16 July 2006

cacophony of sound. Dublin were bidding to retain the title, and thus become the first county to do so in eleven years. Offaly were seeking their first title since 1997.

Dublin may have been favourites and more familiar with the surroundings, but there was a nervous edge to their early play. It was the challengers who made the better start and between them Niall McNamee and Thomas Deehan fired over three points in the opening 12 minutes. In fact it took Dublin 14 minutes to open their account with a Conal Keaney point. Dublin may have looked the more impressive team as the half wore on but for all their movement and more varied threat up front, scores were hard to come by. The champions were dominating in midfield. Ciaran Whelan was outstanding and he had an able assistant in the hard-running Shane Ryan. However, their shooting left a lot to be desired; nine wides in the first half tells its own tale.

The tie was nicely balanced. Offaly, although living off scraps, were still creating chances and were in fact level at 0-6 each when a major talking point in the game arrived, just on half-time. It may

not have been the game's defining moment but it certainly shaped the contest for the second half. And not for the first time in the season the man in the middle, this time Sligo referee Marty Duffy, was central to the decision. Dublin were grateful he showed leniency, Offaly fuming that he flashed yellow when red could just as easily have emerged from his pocket.

Offaly mounted an attack, Cathal Daly was closing in on what looked like a scoring pass. Dublin goalkeeper Stephen Cluxton raced out and ploughed into Daly and hauled him to the ground. In other codes he would have been instantly dismissed, but all Offaly got was a free, Cluxton got a yellow card and the hordes on 'the hill' directly behind the incident could breathe again. To add insult to injury, Niall McNamee hit the resultant free wide. Would this missed opportunity now become the game's defining moment? It meant it was still level as the teams headed for the dressing room at the end of an eventful opening 35 minutes.

Dublin were a transformed team in the second half, even if it was

Tomas Quinn, Dublin, struggles to maintain possession despite the attention of Paul Conway, Offaly. Dublin v Offaly, Leinster Football Final, Croke Park, Dublin. 16 July 2006

Offaly who got the opening point immediately on the restart. But they would add only two more as the Dublin machine clicked into gear. Enter Tomas or Mossy (as he is better known) Quinn. He kicked four unanswered points and it was 0-10 to 0-7 for the champions.

Offaly were wasting chances, some of them from advantageous positions. Coupled with Alan Brogan suddenly finding his range, the challengers were now struggling to stay in touch. To their credit, they kept playing constructive football but undid their hard work with some poor shooting.

Offaly were dealt a further blow in the 53rd minute, when on receipt of a 2nd yellow card Alan McNamee was dismissed.

It seemed to stir them into action, if only briefly, when they landed two quick points. That left it 0-12 to 0-9 with 10 minutes remaining. Crucially, Dublin responded in kind, and the writing was on the wall for the Faithful County.

The game and the title, their 46th, was within Dublin's reach and they finished with a flourish. In the 67th minute, Whelan and Brogan combined to set up Jason Sherlock for the game-clinching goal. Jayo obliged and then added a point to seal a deserved win. With the title in the bag, Dublin manager, Paul Caffrey, emptied the bench, affording the squad members the opportunity to savour the big occasion as the winning margin was extended to 9 points, 1-15 to 0-9.

The result suggests it was a little easier than it actually was. However, there was enough about Dublin's performance to encourage belief that the long wait for that elusive All Ireland title could be about to end.

Offaly will be disappointed at the final outcome. The challenge now was a meeting with neighbours Laois in an effort to prolong their season.

As for Dublin, on the evidence of their surge through Leinster, a Sunday in September beckons.

Leinster Final
Dublin **1-15**
Offaly **0-9**

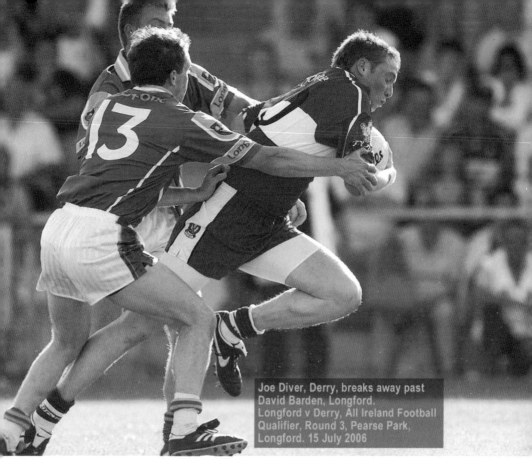

Joe Diver, Derry, breaks away past David Barden, Longford. Longford v Derry, All Ireland Football Qualifier, Round 3, Pearse Park, Longford. 15 July 2006

FOOTBALL QUALIFIERS
Rounds 3 and 4

The Championship heats up as the qualifiers continue. Controversial sending-offs, dramatic departures of big teams, fantastic goals – these qualifiers had it all.

Round 3

Fermanagh	v	Wexford
Meath	v	Laois
Sligo	v	Westmeath
Longford	v	Derry

Four more games on another exciting weekend in the football qualifiers. Glorious weather and big crowds all contributed to the drama and there was plenty of it.

Fermanagh v Wexford

It began before a ball was kicked in the match between Wexford and Fermanagh in Enniskillen. Wexford's Mattie Forde, their best player, was suspended for 12 weeks with immediate effect. This was as a result of an alleged stamping incident in the Leinster semi final. The protracted nature of the proceedings involving Forde angered the Wexford county board, who were only notified of the suspension by email on the morning of the game.

Forde could have attended the meeting of the Central Disciplinary Committee, but chose not to. It left no room for an appeal, he would miss the match.

Wexford struggled without their top scorer. Despite this, the sides were level approaching half-time, when Fermanagh won a penalty. Ciaran O'Reilly struck it confidently into the net and the men from the Erne County were on their way. It was Wexford's third game in 13 days and it told. They were brave and committed, but were eventually undone by Eamonn Maguire's goal, which gave Fermanagh victory by 2-12 to 0-11.

Wexford's season was over, bu there was, and still is, a residue o anger in the Model County ove the handling of the Mattie Ford affair.

Meath v Laois

Páirc Tailteann in Navan was th venue for the all-Leinster clash o Meath and Laois. These grea rivals produced a thriller.

Several times during a pulsatin contest the lead changed hands Meath led early on but wer pegged back by a resilient Laoi side.

Laois were ahead 0-10 to 0-6 a half-time, but in typical Meat fashion the home side clawed thei way back. Twenty-one minute gone in the second half and Meat had regained the lead by a poin Laois had yet to score in th second half. Then enter one Ros Munnelly. This fabulously talented footballer struck tw sublime goals in the space of si minutes. These scores propelle his side into Round 4 as Meat never recovered. It finished Lao 2-13 Meath 0-13. Micko's me march on, Eamonn Barry's fir turbulent year in charge was ove

Sligo v Westmeath

In the shadow of Ben Bulben at Markievicz Park, Sligo and Westmeath met for the first time ever in a Championship encounter and it was laced with drama and controversy. It took extra time to separate the sides, but that masks the real story. Sligo finished with 12 men, Westmeath with 14 and referee Michael Ryan and his officials were the subject of severe criticism after the match. Sligo's best attacker Eamonn O'Hara was at the centre of a controversial sending-off. O'Hara was dismissed on the word of a linesman, and it may very well have been a case of mistaken identity as O'Hara appeared to be at least 22 metres away from the incident. It robbed Sligo of their most potent forward at a crucial stage of the game.

Sligo were in front 0-6 to 0-4 at half-time. However, a resurgent Westmeath gained a grip in the second half and five unanswered points powered them ahead.

Back came Sligo and in a welter of excitement a long-range point earned the Yeats County men a reprieve and forced extra-time.

Paul Bannon, Westmeath, outjumps Sligo's Eamon O'Hara and Tony Taylor, left, Sligo v Westmeath, All Ireland Football Qualifier, Round 3, Markievicz Park, Sligo. 15 July 2006

Approaching the end of extra-time, Sligo despite the numerical disadvantage had eked out a two point lead and looked set for victory. But this dramatic encounter had one final twist and it came in the form of Westmeath's Gary Dolan. Withdrawn earlier in the game, he was re-introduced as an 86th minute substitute.

It proved an inspirational move.

With practically the last kick of the match, he blasted the ball to the net to give Westmeath a victory that hardly did justice to Sligo's brave effort. It was little consolation to Sligo that a few weeks after the game O'Hara had his red card rescinded.

Longford v Derry

The final game of the weekend produced a major shock, although Longford manager Luke Dempsey disagreed with that assessment. A few weeks earlier Longford ran mighty Dublin to just two points. Afterwards the focus was mainly on how poorly Dublin had played. Due credit was not given to Longford. Derry came to town on the back of two impressive wins and were spoken about as serious contenders.

Paddy Bradley was again in outstanding form for Derry and his second goal from a hotly disputed penalty gave his side an interval lead of 2-6 to 1-8. Lesser teams might have folded but this Longford side is made of stern stuff and they produced a fabulous performance to stun the favourites.

Paul Barden was their hero. His point-taking had the teams level at 2-8 to 1-11. A terrific contest never let up. Longford missed several gilt-edged goal opportunities and these wasted chances only added to the excitement. The sides then shared a further eight points, so it was still level heading for injury time. Longford won a long-range free and the ice cool Barden slotted it between the posts for a sensational and deserved winner. Round 4 of the qualifiers may very well be uncharted waters for Longford but they are there on merit. Who knows – could they be the team that will leave an indelible mark on a fascinating series?

The race for Sam was down to 12 counties. With the losing provincial finalists now entering the equation, all eyes were on the draw for this round that would reduce it to eight. What could be described as a marathon, was fast developing into a sprint.

The pairings were intriguing. Kerry v Longford, Laois v Offaly, Galway v Westmeath and Fermanagh v Donegal, with the first named team enjoying home advantage – an important factor at this stage of the Championship.

Kerry v Longford

Kerry and Longford were meeting for the first time in Championship football since the All Ireland semi final of 1968.

It drew a crowd of over 18,000 to Killarney, Kerry's fourth home game of the Championship.

In an obvious reaction to the criticism directed at them after their loss to Cork, Kerry filleted their team for this clash and they were rewarded. Kieran Donaghy wreaked havoc on the Longford defence from the edge of the square, and helped create three first half goals. Eoin Brosnan got two, while newly installed captain

Colm Cooper scored the third. Kerry led 3-7 to 0-7 at half-time.

Longford made an excellent start to the second half but dreadful shooting spoiled their good approach play. Kerry were awarded a penalty in the 53rd minute but Mike Frank Russell's effort was saved by goalkeeper Damien Sheridan. Five minutes later Brian Kavanagh goaled for Longford and there was a glimmer of hope. It was quickly extinguished when Brosnan completed his hat-trick with a final score of Kerry 4-11, Longford 1-11. It sent Kerry to a quarter final meeting with Armagh and a chance to avenge the All Ireland final defeat of 2002, but doubts still persists as to the merits of this Kerry team.

Galway v Westmeath

Westmeath had their meeting with Galway in Pearse Stadium, Tuam. In advance, Ja Fallon came out of retirement and played his first game in three years. Unfortunately, his comeback lasted 10 minutes before being forced off with a shoulder injury.

Westmeath led by 0-6 to 0-4 at half-time but had to face a strong wind in the second half. A superb goal from Gary Dolan 16 minutes from time strengthened their grip on a poor contest.

Galway came forward in waves, cut the lead to one point but despite almost five minutes of added time failed to land the leveller that would have forced extra-time. It ended Westmeath 1-8 Galway 0-10. The men from the Lake County moved on to the last eight of the Championship. This loss possibly heralds the end of an era for Galway football. It certainly provided the shock result for this round of the qualifiers.

Fermanagh v Donegal

The clash of Fermanagh and Donegal in Brewster Park, Enniskillen was another poor affair, a typical Ulster derby in fact.

As with all games over the weekend, the strong wind did not help. It was Fermanagh who had a slender lead 0-5 to 0-3 at half-time but there had been very little for the crowd of 17,893 to get excited about.

Donegal were motivated by the suspension handed out to full-back Paddy Campbell and it showed in their determined approach in the second half. They

eventually reeled Fermanagh in and a couple of late points gave them victory by 0-11 to 0-8 in a best forgotten contest.

In a post-match interview Donegal manager Brian McIver vented his anger over Campbell's suspension at various sources. Among those he targeted were the Central Disciplinary Committee, RTÉ, the Sunday Game panel and even GAA President Nickey Brennan. Nothing like a good row to enliven a dull match. At least it gave the hacks something to write about.

Laois v Offaly

The fare in Portlaoise was not much better as Leinster neighbours Offaly and Laois clashed for the second year in a row.

It was an error-ridden contest with little pattern, but Laois always looked that bit better, even if their half-time lead of 0-5 to 0-3 did not reflect their control. However, in front of a noisy and passionate crowd of 16,800, they chiselled out a merited victory thanks to the industry of a few key players.

It took Offaly 25 minutes to score with the wind in the second

Laois goalkeeper Fergal Byron kicks a penalty over the bar as Offaly goalkeeper Padraig Kelly prepares to dive. Laois v Offaly, All Ireland Football Qualifier, Round 4, O'Moore Park, Portlaoise, Co. Laois. 30 July 2006

half, but any hopes of a comeback were dashed when Ross Munnelly set up Padraig Clancy for the clinching goal in the 61st minute. Laois eventually ran out winners by 1-9 to 0-4 and Offaly's season ends with more questions than answers.

Laois had really improved since their mauling by Dublin. They were aided by a most inept display from Offaly, who amazingly have yet to win a game in the qualifiers.

It was now down to eight. The business end of the Championship and the quarter final pairings made for interesting reading.

Quarter Finals		
Cork	v	Donegal
Kerry	v	Armagh
Dublin	v	Westmeath
Laois	v	Mayo

The big prize was now within touching distance of those still in the race to land Sam.

The outgoing GAA President Sean Kelly pins the presidential badge on to the lapel of the incoming President Nickey Brennan at the 2006 GAA Annual Congress. Great Southern Hotel, Killarney, Co. Kerry. 22 April 2006

SEAN KELLY'S
REIGN AS PRESIDENT

The annual congress of the GAA can at times be a tedious affair, except in the year when the next President of the Association is about to be elected.

That was the case in April 2002 when the assembled delegates chose Sean Kelly to lead them for the next three years.

It was a historic decision; Kelly thus became the first Kerryman to hold the office in the 126 years of the Association's existence.

The three years of the Kilcummin clubman's reign were, to say the least, eventful.

It had its highs and lows but one theme dominated from the outset, Rule 42 or to be more precise the Croke Park affair.

There were others of course. Some good, some bad, but for many Rule 42 defined his presidency. He may not have wished it to be the case, but it did.

Like so many before him, Kelly came through the system, first serving as Chairman of the Kerry county board for ten years. He followed that with a six year stint on the Munster Council, as Vice-Chairman and Chairman.

His election as President was emphatic, thus he took office with a strong mandate to get things done.

He first set about changing the committee system in Croke Park in an effort to streamline and fast track decisions, and his first port of call was the Games Administration Committee (GAC). Kelly felt the group's workload had become too much in recent years. With the addition of the qualifiers in both hurling and football dominating their agenda, along with disciplinary matters, its scope was enormous. His proposal to split the committee in two was at first resisted but it made sense. Now one committee deals with fixtures, while another looks after disciplinary matters. Of course, since the last Congress there are now two further committees who deal with the complicated appeals and disputes procedures.

Hurling was a big concern for Sean and while his background was in football, he made no secret of his desire to see our ancient game revived and he worked hard at this aim. It was his view and one shared by many that the so-called weaker counties deserved support and with it the opportunity to play hurling in the summer months. Hence the Nicky Rackard and Christy Ring Cups saw the light of day. These competitions were the brainchild of the Hurling Development Committee, which Kelly set up. It was the intention that the finals of these competitions would be played in Croke Park as curtain-raisers to All Ireland semi finals. London and Westmeath were the first winners. With live television, the hurlers from the less fashionable counties had their day in the sun. It proved a masterstroke. The manner in which the teams that participated in these competitions embraced them made it all worthwhile. They were an unqualified success.

Football was not ignored and while only five counties entered the Tommy Murphy Cup in the first year, this increased in the following years. It was a source of some joy that the 2005 winners were Tipperary. Fitting then that one of the game's most exciting players, Declan Browne, should climb the steps in Croke Park to receive the cup, a dream fulfilled, that otherwise may never have come to pass. For that he can thank Sean Kelly.

The lowest point could well be the initial failure to get Rule 42 on the agenda for Congress and the manner in which it was blocked – by the motions committee, a committee comprised of ex-Presidents of the GAA – was technically correct. In order to ensure the motion would at least get an airing a year later, Kelly set about changing the terms of reference of the 'motions committee'.

It was his view that if ordinary club members wanted something discussed at Congress there was an obligation on the Association to allow it to happen.

A Special Congress was imminent and he availed of the opportunity to get the system changed. It meant motions that heretofore were deemed out of order could be resubmitted in their proper form. The first, and at times the most difficult, hurdle had been cleared.

Sean then spoke to counties who had already taken a decision and asked them to revisit the situation again on the basis that Croke Park would only be opened on a temporary basis while Lansdowne Road was out of commission.

The move for change quickly gathered momentum, even if some counties remained trenchant in their opposition, among them Cork, New York and a number of Ulster counties. New York's view was 'demoralising' according to Kelly, especially when as a unit they are dependent on so many other bodies for facilities to promote the games in a city where there are many problems to overcome.

Despite the gathering momentum, he was unsure if the two-thirds majority could be achieved, that is until he was handed the slip of paper. Tá 200 Níl 97. The former St Brendan's, Killarney schoolteacher did not need a degree in maths to work out the implications. Croke Park would open its gates to other sports. Kelly's legacy was assured.

The debate over, the Association quickly united behind the

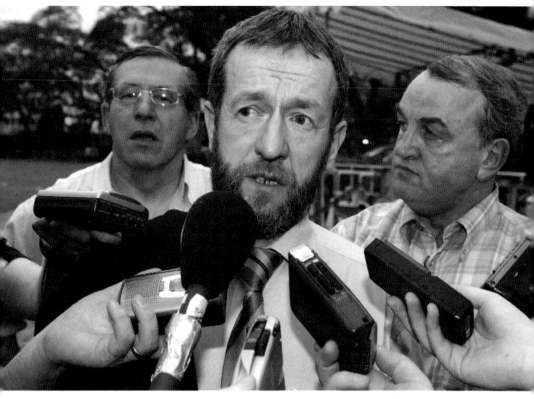

Liam Mulvihill, Ard Stuirthoir, left, Sean Kelly, President, Nickey Brennan, President Elect of the GAA, at a 'Press Briefing' after the Vodafone GAA All-Stars Exhibition Game. Singapore Polo Club, Singapore. 21 January 2006

decision, even people within those counties who were opposed to the rule change. It was said to him on more then one occasion, 'Sean, we were against it but we debated it and now we accept the decision and we move on'.

Not everyone though was as magnanimous. Famously Ulster Council Chairman Miceal Greenan made a very public stand at the conclusion of Kelly's last speech as President. The Congress was held in Killarney to coincide with the end of Sean Kelly's term of office. The delegates to a man gave the outgoing Uachtarán a standing ovation. Greenan though stayed seated and did not join in the applause or plaudits being handed out to Kelly.

Greenan, a highly respected official in the Association, refused to be, in his words 'a hypocrite'. He said, 'I received a lot of support for my stand from all over the country and that includes Kerry'.

The Ulster Council Chairman took issue with some aspects of Kelly's presidency, in particular Croke Park, but the two men were to later shake hands and like everyone else move on.

It would be wrong to focus solely on the Croke Park debate. Sean also wanted the update of Croke Park brought to its conclusion.

Hill 16 and the Northern end were completed on time and within budget. There are other areas that Kelly had an enormous impact: securing the €40 million grant from the Government, improvement of player welfare, including greater and more harmonious dialogue with the Gaelic Players Association. He also oversaw the development of the new Croke Park Hotel, and encouraged the progression of the integration between the GAA and the Ladies' Football and Camogie Associations.

A short few years ago the club championships were expanded at provincial and national level to include Junior and Intermediate grades. These finals are now played in Croke Park, something Sean Kelly advocated on their introduction.

Kelly usually moved at a faster pace than people expected. In an attempt to speed up matters, all his sub-committees were given particular terms of reference for just one year. 'It was a system that enabled me to get a lot of things done,' he said.

Kelly's tenure at the helm was one of accessibility, whereby he

Sean Kelly, President, GAA.
2003 – 2006

was revered by the grassroots, but in the little offices within Croke Park they were constantly second guessing his movements as his media profile took off. His phone number was readily available to anyone that sought it. Unless it was improper to do so, he always answered or immediately returned calls.

In three years he covered almost 50,000 miles a year, mostly driving himself, often alone. He visited clubs and clubhouses in all parts of the country, and each visit holds a special memory. Some stand out more than others, one such memory will stay with him for some time to come.

Having attended a function in Gweedore, County Donegal one evening, the following night he was due in Doonbeg, County Clare for a similar event. The alarm was set for early next morning, a long drive ahead. Leaving Gweedore, the sun was shining and very few had risen from their beds as he set out on his journey. He then noticed activity in the local GAA field. It was littered with young boys kicking a football. In their midst were two adults. Sean pulled the car into the field and walked towards the

adults supervising the session. As he drew closer he recognised them as Tony Boyle and Declan Bonner, two outstanding forwards of their generation. But such was their interest in the young kids they barely noticed the President of the GAA was walking among them.

It was to be an all day session, but later that evening Bonner and Boyle would be in direct opposition when their respective clubs collided in the county championship.

It left a lasting impression on Kelly; 'here you had two brilliant footballers giving of their time and energy ensuring the next group of young footballers in their county would get the best possible coaching. That tells me our Association is in safe hands. And it's a situation that is replicated at playing fields up and down the country, the grassroots of the GAA.'

It's to the grassroots that Sean Kelly returned in April of this year, when Kilkenny's Nickey Brennan took over the reins of office at Congress. Given Kelly's commitment no doubt he will remain active at some level for many years to come.

In the intervening period, he has taken on a new role as the Irish Institute of Sport's Executive Chairman.

Throughout his three years at the helm of the country's largest sporting organisation, Sean received unstinting support from his wife Juliet and family Muiread, Sean, Padraig and Laurence. Now as a degree of normality returns to the Kelly household in Kilcummin, it's time to move on. But Kelly would never be able to go back to teaching after the exploits and success of his reign in the GAA hot seat and it was only a matter of time before a big job came his way.

Soon after, such is his massive profile, he was asked to be a judge for the Rose of Tralee pageant. That's Kelly to a tee, an administrator with the highest ambition who made his name with the common touch.

Eoin Hannon, Kildare, tries to take the ball past Brendan Delargy, Antrim. Christy Ring Cup Semi Final, Kildare v Antrim, Cusack Park, Mullingar, Co. Westmeath. 23 July 2006

CHRISTY RING & NICKY RACKARD CUPS

The descision to give the 'weaker' hurling counties their own competition was an inspired one. Naming the Cups after the two greatest exponents of the game was a wonderful gesture.

The Hurling Development Committee's innovative decision to give the so-called weaker hurling counties their own competition was an inspired one. Naming the cups after two of the greatest exponents of the ancient game was also a fantastic gesture and the presence of the Ring and Rackard families at the inaugural finals in 2005 reflected this.

The principal idea behind the 'cups' was to provide these 'weaker' counties with their own meaningful competitions. It allowed them to play at a time of year that was conducive to hurling. Hitherto, many of these teams would have been confined to playing winter hurling. It also ensured that for the very first time, all 32 counties plus London and Warwickshire were active in competitive fare right into July.

However, the early rounds of this year's competitions were of little value to the participants, simply because of the one-sided nature of the games.

CHRISTY RING CUP

There was a big surprise in the first round of the Christy Ring Cup when Antrim were beaten by Down 1-23 to 1-7, reversing their Ulster championship result. London made a great start to the competition by winning their first two games, putting themselves in contention for a semi final place.

Roscommon felt the backlash from Down's victory over Antrim and were hammered by Antrim in the second round. The scoreboard made for depressing reading for the men from the West, Antrim 9-39 Roscommon 0-5.

Kerry, who had reached the Division 2 league final, were hoping to make an impact in this

competition. However, the opposite occurred, and they failed to make the knockout stages.

There were rumours of dissatisfaction with manager James Moyleneaux. In the end, Kerry lost all four games and were plunged into a relegation battle with Roscommon. Defeat would see the losers drop to the Nicky Rackard Cup for 2007.

Roscommon's plight was just as bad and to avoid the embarrassment of conceding a walkover, selector Anthony Flaherty was forced out of retirement a week earlier for the game against Meath. It came as no surprise that Kerry won the play-off game and Roscommon were relegated.

London's early promise faded and when the dust settled on the uninspiring group stages, the semi final pairings emerged.

Down would meet Carlow, and Antrim, having recovered from their initial loss, would face Kildare who were rank outsiders before the competition began.

The semi finals produced two games of contrasting fortunes. Antrim rode roughshod over Kildare and long before the finish the outcome was decided. Liam

Watson contributed 12 points for the men from the 'Glens' who won as they pleased. The final score tells its own tale, Antrim 2-21 Kildare 0-6.

It was generally expected that Ulster rivals Down would provide the opposition in the final, but Carlow had other ideas.

The outsiders built up a commanding interval lead of 0-12 to 0-4 despite hitting 14 wides. Down staged a storming second half comeback inspired by the brilliance of Paul Branniff who scored 4-6 of his side's total. Down actually took a 3 point lead but Carlow displayed great resilience and Dan Murphy drilled in two goals.

It was now a two point game as Down came forward in search of the winning goal. Carlow though held firm and in a welter of excitement hung on for a narrow win by 2-19 to 5-8.

The full-time whistle was greeted with wild excitement and for the second time in a matter of months a team from the county with the distinctive yellow, green and red jerseys would grace Croke Park on a big day for hurling. Keep in mind, though, that the Carlow minors did reach the Leinster Final, so maybe it wasn't that big a surprise after all.

It was to be an unusual pairing then for the Christy Ring Cup Final on August 6th, Carlow v Antrim.

Carlow v Antrim

In advance of the final, there was a view among hurling people that Antrim were too strong for this competition.

The decider played as a curtain-raiser to the

Joey Scullion, Antrim, in action against Carlow. Christy Ring Cup Final, Antrim v Carlow, Croke Park, Dublin. 6 August 2006

Cork v Waterford semi final was virtually all over after fifteen minutes and held little appeal for those neutrals watching. The result clearly exposed a weakness in the GAA's hurling structure and will surely prompt a rethink for next season.

As it was, Antrim won as they pleased, the winning margin was 21 points as Carlow's limitations, despite a brave effort, were cruelly exposed.

With 18 minutes played, it was 3-7 to 0-0 and Antrim's greater stick work and speed of thought was way above anything Carlow could muster.

Joey Scullion, Johnny McIntosh and Kieran Kelly scored the goals and at the break it was 3-7 to 0-2. Damien Roberts finally opened Carlow's account in the 28th minute.

The second half was a tepid affair. Antrim, content the title was in the bag, strolled through a listless 35 minutes and had further goals from McIntosh and Brian McFall.

Goalkeeper Frank Foley did get a late Carlow goal from a penalty, but it made little difference to the final result, Antrim 5-13 Carlow 1-7.

Antrim will contest the Liam McCarthy Cup in 2007, but as an exercise they learned little in this competition. As for Carlow, they learned that the gap between big and small still exists.

NICKY RACKARD CUP

This is the third tier of competition and similar to the Christy Ring Cup, the early rounds were notable for the one-sided nature of some of the matches.

John O'Dwyer, Derry, in action against James Callaghan, Donegal. Nicky Rackard Cup Final, Derry v Donegal, Croke Park, Dublin. 12 August 2006

GAA President Nickey Brennan attended one of the group games between Leitrim and Louth, played on a pristine surface in Ballinamona club grounds. He was fulsome in his praise for the efforts of both teams. Nickey, a former inter-county player and manager, assured the participating teams of the Association's continued support and promotion for these competitions.

There were three groups in this competition. While some games were of poor quality, the honesty and effort of the participants was never in doubt.

Donegal and Sligo emerged from Group 3A, Armagh and Louth from 3B, with Derry and Longford topping 3C. Derry's plight was interesting as not so long ago they were Ulster champions. Now they were in a rebuilding phase. They had taken the first steps to recovery by making the play-off stages of the Nicky Rackard Cup.

Armagh, Derry and Donegal went straight to the semi finals, leaving Longford, Sligo and Louth to determine the last spot.

Longford defeated Sligo by 1-18 to 1-13,

to set up a quarter final clash with Louth which they won to complete the semi final line up.

Derry's rehabilitation continued when they proved too good for fellow Ulster side Armagh in their semi final. First half goals from Ruairi Convery and Sean McBride put Derry in control. Armagh were hampered by an injury to top scorer Declan Coulter. His absence weakened their attack. Derry sealed victory and a place in the final when McBride grabbed their third goal in a 3-10 to 0-10 win.

Donegal ensured it would be an all-Ulster final when they easily accounted for Longford in the second semi final. There was never much doubt about the outcome and Niall Campbell's 26th minute goal helped his side to an emphatic 1-19 to 0-10 win.

So in an unusual setting, it's the hurlers of Derry and Donegal who would contest the Nicky Rackard Cup final as a curtain-raiser to Dublin and Westmeath in football.

Derry v Donegal

Derry justified their favourite's tag as they defeated Donegal to take the Nicky Rackard Cup and

Antrim captain Karl McKeegan lifts the Christy Ring cup at the end of the game. Antrim v Carlow, Christy Ring Cup Final, Croke Park, Dublin. 6 August 2006

in the process secure their place in the Christy Ring Cup for 2007. It was no real surprise that they won this tie and there was not even the merest hint of a shock. Brave as Donegal were, they simply lacked the experience and craft of their more seasoned opponents although to their credit they battled away to the end.

Indeed were it not for a few careless moments in defence Donegal would have been much closer at the finish. They were doing well in midfield and their ability to take some long-range scores kept them in touch.

Derry struck for two goals in the second quarter, and both could have been prevented. Ruairí Convery's 65 dropped short and the inability of two defenders to deal with it allowed the ball to sail into the top corner of the net. Undaunted, Donegal scored the next two points, but were undone again with the half-time break in sight.

Goalkeeper Gerard Grindle made a great save from Kevin Hinphey. However, he failed to execute an effective clearance and Convery was on hand to tap in a simple goal.

Niall Campbell gave Donegal

hope with a goal early in the second half as a result of some neat build-up play, but they failed to maintain the momentum and Derry soon turned the screw.

Derry's third goal arrived courtesy of Sean McBride who then went on to complete his hat-trick as the scoreboard took on a lopsided look that scarcely reflected Donegal's efforts. In the end, Derry won comprehensively by 5-15 to 1-11, and it was a proud captain Michael Conway who accepted the cup from GAA President Nickey Brennan. Sadly, this game was played out in a near-deserted Croke Park as the majority of the 79,000 who attended the Dublin v Westmeath football game chose to socialise rather than watch a hurling game. The players from both sides deserved better.

It is somewhat ironic that in a year when the football fraternity from Ulster return with an empty cupboard, two hurling titles went their way north. Proof if it was ever needed that the ancient game continues to enjoy huge support among the hurling fraternity in a proud province. They may be small in numbers, but they are big in heart and commitment.

Neil Ronan, Cork, strikes the ball despite the attempted 'hook' by Barry Foley, Limerick. Cork v Limerick, All Ireland Hurling Quarter Final, Semple Stadium, Thurles, Co. Tipperary. 22 July 2006

HURLING EXTRAVAGANZA

Quarter-Final Action in the Hurling Championships

Surprises, disappointments and some testing moments for the teams in the quarter-finals of the Guinness Hurling Championships. Not all the pairings produced magical matches, but at least one did . . .

Quarter Finals

Cork	v	Limerick
Kilkenny	v	Galway
Clare	v	Wexford
Waterford	v	Tipperary

It would surely come to life now. The top eight teams in the country were going head to head on a July weekend, when reputations and records counted for little. There is no disguising the fact that even at this stage, the Guinness All Ireland Hurling Championship had yet to ignite.

Leinster was as predictable as a government budget in election year. Ulster did not even get to play a final. Connacht's sole representatives, Galway, only joined the race in the qualifiers. That left Munster. The province was still basking in the success of the rugby team winning the Heineken Cup as the Championship kicked in.

The quarter final pairings made for an intriguing weekend of action. Even before a ball was struck in anger, there was anger. Galway were annoyed at having to travel to Thurles for a 6pm start on a Saturday against Kilkenny. The men from the west were far from happy.

Cork were paired against Limerick, a team slowly recovering its soul after a traumatic few months. The all-Munster pairing would get underway at 4.15pm.

Twenty-four hours later Croke Park would be the centre of attention for yet another double header. Clare and Wexford, with the eagerly awaited rematch of Tipperary and Waterford due to follow.

Hurling supporters were hoping these four games would at least rescue a Championship that badly needed an infusion of oxygen to spark it into life. Sadly, what materialised was just one good game out of four. Serious questions have to be asked of the standard in some counties.

Cork v Limerick

It was a strange feeling to be in Thurles on a Saturday afternoon. There were initial fears that the venue would not cope with the expected crowd. As it was, it comfortably held the 34,202, which is close to the figure that Croke Park officials estimated would attend.

All Ireland champions Cork were first into action against Munster rivals Limerick, who were rank outsiders with bookmakers and pundits alike.

There was a cutting edge to Limerick's play in the opening stages as they matched the champions score for score. In advance, manager Ritchie Bennis had promised a return to basics from his side which would test Cork. His team responded but there was a lack of discipline at times. They conceded needless frees, for which they were duly punished by Cork.

the second half if they were to have any chance of causing an upset, but there was little indication that it would happen.

Cork had moved 0-15 to 0-8 ahead and a semi final spot loomed on the horizon. However, as the rain came, so did Limerick and they enjoyed their best spell of the match. Suddenly Cork were on the ropes.

Niall Moran and Pat Tobin had a brace of points

With 25 minutes played it was level 0-5 to 0-5. Gradually, there was a noticeable improvement in Cork's play. Several key battles were going their way. Diarmuid Sullivan put the shackles on Brian Begley, while Brian Murphy kept a tight rein on Andrew O'Shaughnessy.

In the period before the break Cork cut loose and they hit six points. Tom Kenny and Niall Ronan had two each while Niall McCarthy and Ben O'Connor had one apiece. Limerick's only reply was an O'Shaughnessy point from a free. That left Cork 0-11 to 0-6 in front at half-time. Having weathered the anticipated early challenge from Limerick, it was all going to plan.

Limerick needed a good start to

each, Conor Fitzgerald and O'Shaughnessy also contributed and now the gap was the bare minimum. Cork 0-15 Limerick 0-14.

Deane and Ben O'Connor missed frees, and Cork looked in trouble. They refused to panic though. O'Connor nailed a long-range free, Brian Corcoran was fouled and Deane tapped the resultant penalty over the bar: 0-17 to 0-14 for Cork.

In truth, it was a pretty poor contest for the most part, but it was suddenly illuminated by a dramatic finish. In the final two minutes of normal time plus three minutes added for stoppages, the sides shared six points.

Limerick may have got four of them, but crucially they never gained parity and Cork held on for the narrowest of wins.

Donal Óg Cusack's puck out was the last act of a dramatic encounter and the champions had survived. Their three-in-a-row ambitions were still alive, just barely at 0-19 to 0-18.

Kilkenny v Galway

In the 2005 Championship the game of the year was the semi final clash of Kilkenny and Galway which the latter won, with a glut of goals. Now they were set to do battle again, this time in the quarter final. Could Galway repeat their heroics?

Kilkenny, with a reshaped team from the Leinster final, were in full flow from the start and ran Galway ragged. In a breathtaking opening 35 minutes they scored at will and looked unbeatable. Cha Fitzpatrick scored a rather fortuitous goal that will haunt Galway goalkeeper Liam O'Donoghue for some time to come. Aidan Fogarty kicked home a second goal and with Henry Shefflin firing over some spectacular points, Kilkenny led 2-13 to 0-6 at half-time. It was a shell-shocked Galway side that trooped off discontentedly for the sanctuary of the dressing room, wondering how to retrieve a seemingly hopeless position.

Conor Hayes rang the changes for the second half. Eugene Cloonan, Richie Murray and David Tierney entered the fray. Many were wondering why some of these players were not on from the very start. This was given further credence by the displays these players produced, as they clawed their way back into the game.

There was little change to the pattern of the contest as the half wore on. Niall Healy flicked in a Galway goal to give them hope, while Eugene Cloonan was causing trouble for the Kilkenny defence. But at double scores 2-18 to 1-9, Galway's cause looked a lost one. That is until Kilkenny were reduced to fourteen men when Derek Lyng was dismissed following a second yellow card.

Galway knocked over a couple of points and suddenly the evening's consignment of fireworks arrived as Kilkenny briefly looked vulnerable.

Two minutes after Lyng's sending-off, David Tierney crashed in a Galway goal. Then they had a third 'goal' from David Forde, but it was correctly disallowed for a square infringement.

Cloonan drilled in a penalty on 65 minutes and the gap was now down to five points. Could they complete a memorable comeback and fashion a win from a seemingly hopeless position? Kilkenny steadied the ship and slipped over a couple of points to finally kill off the Galway challenge. At one point, Kilkenny led by 17 points. Galway's pride eventually reduced the final margin to five, but time ran out and the Leinster champions staggered into the semi final.

What seemed like a procession at one stage ended in a frenetic finish, with Kilkenny winning by 2-22 to 3-14.

A romp and a thriller.

Clare v Wexford

For the second successive year, Clare and Wexford met in the last eight. In truth this game ceased to be a meaningful contest in the 11th minute when Clare's Diarmuid McMahon rattled in a goal to put his side 1-7 to 0-1 ahead.

It was all one way traffic in the direction of the Wexford goal. It was hard to believe it was an All Ireland quarter final; at times it resembled a challenge match. Clare led 1-13 to 0-7 at half time.

There was little to get excited about in the second half. Anthony Daly used his full compliment of substitutes as they romped to a staggering 1-27 to 1-15 win. It was a stroll in the afternoon sun for Clare. It left the early arrivals in the 45,928 crowd at HQ with little to enthuse about. Wexford were simply not at the races and the passion and commitment associated with their play was sadly lacking. The result raises serious question marks about the state of the game in Wexford. Under-age success is now but a distant memory and they are slowly slipping down the pecking order. Remedial action is needed and needed quickly to save a

Shane McGrath, Tipperary, prevents the ball reaching Shane O'Sullivan, Waterford.
Tipperary v Waterford, All Ireland Hurling Quarter Final, Croke Park, Dublin. 23 July 2006

proud county from further slippage.

As for Clare they strolled into the semi final with little fuss and looked impressive as they disposed of the tissue-like resistance offered by Wexford. They could do no more.

Tipperary v Waterford

It is often said that at a party, the best wine is kept until last. The best did at last surface and for that Tipperary and Waterford deserve credit. Were it not for their efforts, it would have been a far less exciting weekend.

When the sides met in the

Munster championship, Waterford were ravaged by injury and taken apart by the brilliance of Eoin Kelly. On this occasion they had both a full playing complement of players and the game plan to limit Kelly's effectiveness.

It was a match that had pace and power all over the field and supplemented with some outstanding individual displays, most of them in the blue and white of Waterford.

Waterford got the opening point, but then John Carroll drilled in a fabulous goal to give Tipperary the lead they held for the majority of the first half.

Dan Shanahan was in sparkling form for Waterford and struck some majestic points from all angles, he was superb.

Tipperary, though, still led and when Eoin Kelly drove a powerful free to the net, one wondered would it be another disappointing day in Dublin for the 'Decies'.

The tide turned just before the break. Shanahan was fouled in the square and Ken McGrath's free was deflected over for a point by Brendan Cummins. Crucially, it gave Waterford a slender but deserved lead of 0-13 to 2-6 at half-time.

It also gave them renewed confidence for the second half and they were further boosted when Shanahan scored a goal of sheer class in the 43rd minute (he finished with 1-5 from play). Waterford had now gone seven points ahead and were full value for that lead. Tipperary were struggling as the Waterford half-back line produced a quality performance, especially Ken McGrath.

Babs reshuffled his pack and the introduction of Willie Ryan helped, but Waterford still held the initiative. With five minutes remaining, Tipperary were given a glimmer of hope when John Carroll knocked in their third goal. The gap was now a mere three points – not a true reflection of the difference between the teams, as Tipperary harboured hopes of forcing a replay However, their efforts were thwarted by the excellence of the Waterford defence, in particular McGrath. He diverted a blistering drive from Kelly out for a '65' that he then caught and cleared to end Tipperary's ambitions for another year and rid themselves of the Croke Park hoodoo that dates back to July 1998.

That just left four teams standing as Sean Fogarty and Rory Sheridan presided over the semi final draw. Champions Cork would face Waterford, with Kilkenny meeting Clare.

It had been billed as a weekend of hurling extravaganza, but it was hardly that. There were just three games left in the 2006 Hurling Championship and it really needed a lift. Could the semi finals provide it? Hopefully they would.

The Sam Maguire Cup (the trophy presented to the Winners of the All Ireland Football Championship). On display in Croke Park, Dublin, 14 Sept 1997.

A PRECIOUS CARGO
Cuthbert Donnelly, Keeper of 'Sam'

'Sam's' keeper offers an insight into the busy life of the GAA's most prized piece of silverware.

It's 9.15am. Cuthbert Donnelly and his family are just sitting down to breakfast, when the phone rings. It will be first of many calls.

'Good morning', . . . 'yes, this is Cuthbert Donnelly, how can I help you?' The family members glance at each other. They are only too well aware of what is coming next. It is yet another request for a visit from 'Sam'.

The 'Sam' referred to is the most famous cup in Gaelic football, the Sam Maguire Cup, resident in Tyrone now for the second time in three years.

To be more precise, its residency is the Donnelly household, a few short miles from the village of Aughnacloy.

When Tyrone captain Brian Dooher accepted the cup from Sean Kelly on the 25th of September 2005, one man knew exactly what lay in store for him over the coming months.

That man is Cuthbert Donnelly. So who exactly is Cuthbert Donnelly?

He is a former chairman of the Tyrone county board and currently its representative on the Ulster Council. He is also chairman of his club Aghaloo O'Neill's in Aughnacloy, a position he has held for the last 27 years. He has had a lifelong involvement with the GAA. Married to Mary Mullen from Flintona, he has two sons Michael (34) and Stephen (26). Stephen's wedding was set for July of this year, 2006, and therein lies another tale.

The story really began in 2003 when Tyrone won their first title. Such was the huge volume of requests for the cup that the county board decided to enlist Cuthbert's help.

Since then, wherever 'Sam' goes Cuthbert goes. It's a case of 'have Sam will travel'.

Planes, trains and automobiles have been used to ferry the cup to weddings, wakes and christenings, be they in the North, South, East or West of the country.

Far-off shores too have been visited – New York, San Francisco, Atlanta, Toronto, Ottawa and Halifax in Nova Scotia among them.

Closer to home, cities in England, Scotland and Cardiff in Wales (for the very first time), have all enjoyed Cuthbert and the cup for a few hours.

No request is refused unless the logistics don't add up. Australia and New Zealand are out and the rules laid down are simple – no payment and no alcohol.

It has become a labour of love for Cuthbert and when the time comes to hand it back, he will miss it: 'I know the call will come from Croke Park, and I will miss it when that happens, I can be sure of that,' he says.

Over the years there have been some strange requests. For instance, on a visit to Philadelphia, he was asked to bring Sam along to 'a viewing', the equivalent of an Irish wake.

Cuthbert tells the story that '. . . for over an hour, the cup was placed at the head of the coffin on a pedestal and as people filed by to pay their respects to the deceased they would touch the cup on the way out. It was a most amazing sight.' There are many such similar stories, especially in his native county.

One such visit left him visibly moved. He returned home at 4.30am in the morning after attending a function in Leitrim. Within five hours he was turning the ignition of the car and steering it in the direction of a hospice in Derry. It was a journey he was not looking forward to, more out of tiredness then anything else.

'Many of the patients in the hospice hadn't long to live but for the few minutes that Sam was with them, they lit up. It meant something to them. It was a diversion from their fight for life. It brought tears to my eyes and I can tell you my mood on the way home was a lot different,' he recalls.

The first ever visit of Sam to Cardiff was also special, so special in fact it was covered by national television. Part of the airport was closed for its arrival so the whole process could be filmed.

It was on then to meet the Irish community in the city and the welcome they received there was one of the best ever. Cuthbert explains, 'there were three large banners announcing our arrival and then a huge crowd greeted us before we went upstairs for a question and answer session that lasted nearly two hours, it was fantastic.'

At the function later in the evening, Cuthbert received another request. This time it was from a priest serving on the other side of the city and dealing with a non-Irish community. Would he bring the cup to mass the following morning? Ever the gentleman, he obliged.

The priest then devoted a large part of his sermon to Sam and what it meant to the Irish people. The congregation were fascinated at the story behind Sam.

Since September, Cuthbert and Sam have clocked up close to

60,000 miles which includes about seven or eight transatlantic flights.

Has he ever lost what Páidí O'Sé once called 'the canister'? With all the travelling through airports, it must be a worry. 'There have been a few close calls but so far so good, but I have one golden rule when travelling by plane. I never get off until I can see the 'cup' emerging from the luggage compartment.'

But others are not so careful. Earlier in the year Peter Canavan and Philip Jordan took the cup to Luton for a function. All went well until they returned to Belfast. On arrival there was no sign of Sam.

Cuthbert spent a frantic night calling Belfast and Luton. Eventually Sam was located; in fact it never left Luton Airport in the first place.

Travelling with the cup has been made easier by the special and unique casing that O'Neill's Sports designed for Sam. 'Once I see that then it's okay.'

Cuthbert considers it his and Tyrone's duty to accede to most requests for the cup. It is, he said, 'our duty, Sam does not belong to anyone or any particular county.

Cuthbert Donnelly – Keeper of the Precious Trophy – the Sam Maguire Cup from September 2005 to July 2006

We (Tyrone) are simply the current caretakers. It is such an inspirational force it could prompt a group of wee boys to win an All Ireland medal in the years to come and bring it to their own county as champions for the first time.'

Despite the fact that Cuthbert is now into his 65th year, his commitment and enthusiasm for the role is undiminished and he displays the vitality of a starry-eyed child in his work. It has also brought its own reward, not that he ever sought any.

In 2005, he was the recipient of a President's Award from Sean Kelly and on St Patrick's Day, 2006, he was honoured by the Tyrone Society of New York.

At the 115th annual dinner dance held in Crystal Palace, New York, Cuthbert was named 'Tyrone Man of the Year', a supreme accolade from the men and women of the 'Red Hand County' domiciled in that famous city. It was a fantastic night as a huge crowd attended the event to honour Cuthbert and Sam. It is a night Cuthbert will never forget. 'It was a wonderful occasion and I felt privileged to be honoured by people from my own county, who for various reasons had to leave Ireland but are still great supporters of our games, and the joy they got at seeing the Sam Maguire Cup made it all worthwhile. It was an experience that will live with me for a long time to come,' Cuthbert said as he recalled with pride an emotional night in the city that never sleeps.

Cuthbert's son Stephen was busy making the arrangements for his wedding in July 2006 and kept reminding his dad of the date. Cuthbert then asked Stephen, 'Do you want the cup at the wedding?' to which Stephen replied, 'No dad, but I want you there; Make sure the date is kept free.' He did and the wedding went off without a hitch, and yes, as you would expect, Sam did make an appearance.

It has been an eventful journey for Cuthbert and one that he has enjoyed immensely. But like all journeys, it has a beginning and an end and this one is nearing its destination.

Tyrone's grip on the cup was loosened by Laois on a wet and windy Saturday in July, as Cuthbert sat in the stand in O'Moore Park, Portlaoise. Naturally he was disappointed to see his beloved Tyrone exit the championship, but at least now he will in his own words 'get to enjoy a few dinners in my own home for a change over the coming months.'

Before that though a number of remaining engagements must be fulfilled. Very soon the telephone in the Donnelly household will ring (some say it never stops!) and this time it will be from Croke Park. The request will come,

'Cuthbert, can we have our Cup back.'

It will be returned, probably with a heavy heart but with the certainty that it was in good hands for the last few months. It has brought joy and happiness to so many in that time, all because of the dedication and commitment of Cuthbert Donnelly, a man apart in Tyrone GAA and beyond.

The wet and windy day in July 2006 that Cuthbert Donnelly learned that 'Sam' would not be returning to Tyrone in September 2006. Darren Rooney and Tom Kelly, Laois, try to catch Colm McCullagh, Tyrone. Laois v Tyrone, All Ireland Football Qualifier, Round 2, O'Moore Park, Portlaoise, Co. Laois. 8 July 2006

Offaly's Pascal Kellaghan talks to referee Michael Hughes before being shown the yellow card. Kildare v Offaly, Leinster Football, Quarter Final, Croke Park, Dublin. 28 May 2006

The
BLOOD SUB RULE

The Blood Sub rule has caused controversy since its inception. A Kildare v Offaly Leinster Championship match in May 2006 became the catalyst for another debate on this troublesome issue.

Offaly v Kildare

Sunday, May 28, 2006

With 15 minutes gone in the Bank of Ireland Leinster Football Championship tie between Offaly and Kildare, Offaly introduced James Coughlan as a blood substitute. The player he replaced was Pascal Kellaghan. All was in order so far. However, as events transpired it sparked a controversy that led to a series of appeals before the result of the game could finally be confirmed.

Kellaghan resumed his position for the second half, but it was Trevor Phelan who came off and not Coughlan. This was interpreted by many as a full substitution rather than a 'blood sub'.

The situation was further complicated when 69 minutes into the game, Offaly brought on James Keane. Kildare contended that this was the sixth substitute Offaly had used – one more than what is permitted by the rules.

Kildare were further incensed because they had used their full quota of substitutes and were forced to play the last 10 minutes with 14 men after an injury to one of their players.

Offaly won a tight contest by 3-9 to 0-15 watched by a fine crowd of 32,337. However, the supporters had barely left the stadium when it emerged that there could be a problem with the result.

The Offaly management were adamant that they had stuck to the rules, and this view was supported by Croke Park officials, including the fourth official on duty at the game. In fact, his assistant that day, Pierce Freaney, was convinced Offaly had acted correctly, saying 'Offaly used five substitutes and one blood substitute and this is within the rules, so there is no problem'.

However, the Leinster Council, obviously concerned about the situation, issued a statement within hours of the game finishing. Its content cast doubt about both the actual result and whether Offaly or Kildare would advance to the semi final.

The Council said they were aware of the uncertainty surrounding the introduction of substitutes during the game and would consider all the facts in the coming days. Indeed, a full Leinster Council meeting was called for Monday May 29th, 24 hours after the game. Representatives of both counties were invited to attend.

Since its introduction, the blood sub rule has been dogged with controversy. A number of high profile games have been the subject of appeals and investigations following disputes involving the interpretation of this rule.

Kildare were actually relegated to Division 2 of the league a few years ago as a result of having two points deducted for using one substitute too many in a game against Sligo. Cork encountered difficulties in a Munster Football Final with Tipperary at a stage when they were ahead by 20 points!

At club level, Navan O'Mahoneys used one extra substitute in a Meath championship win over Dunboyne. Dunboyne appealed, were successful and were awarded the game – a decision later upheld by the Leinster Council and the Disputes Resolution Authority (DRA).

The Dunboyne manager that day was Gerry Quinn, who on Sunday was the stand-in Offaly manager for the suspended Kevin Kilmurray.

In this latest controversy, speculation was rife as to the outcome and possible ramifications for both counties. It was a headache the Leinster Council could have done without.

There was even a suggestion that Offaly could be removed from the Championship and Kildare, who lost the match, could not, under the rules, be awarded the game. This would result in Wexford, who were awaiting the winners in the semi final, getting a very easy passage into the final!

Unlikely some said, but possible. However, events took another turn at Monday's Leinster Council meeting.

The meeting which lasted for two hours failed to reach a decision and referred the matter, for clarification, to the Central Council, which was scheduled to meet the following Saturday in Croke Park. It was a matter they did not expect to have on their agenda.

Kildare by now had also held a full county board meeting and while they were at pains to stress that they did not want Offaly removed from the Championship, the officers were granted permission to pursue the matter as far as possible. According to Kildare chairman Sly Merrins, i was 'the least they owed thei players'.

Offaly meanwhile were adaman that they would contest the sem final and reserved comment until all the relevant bodies had ruled on the matter, which was now the dominant subject in all strands of the sports media. In the only comment attributed to an Offaly official, Secretary Christy Todd said, 'nobody can actually show us a rule we are supposed to have broken, we made five substitutions and one substitution under the blood rule.

There is no way we can lose the game on that basis.'

There was a series of meetings on the June weekend as efforts were made to bring finality to the situation. First up was the all-powerful Management Committee of the GAA who met on Friday June 2nd. They issued a directive to the Central Council meeting the following day.

The Management Committee examined a number of rulings and decided that a technicality was in place which meant that the Leinster Council had to make a ruling as they (the Leinster Council) were the body responsible for the fixture and should not have sent it to the Central Council for clarification.

Colm Quinn, Offaly, tries to retain possession despite the attention of Killian Brennan, Kildare. Kildare v Offaly, Leinster Football, Quarter Final, Croke Park, Dublin. 28 May 2006

It was the view of the Management Committee that if the Central Council ruled on the matter, it could be seen as 'definitive', while under current procedures both counties had the right of appeal.

This was accepted by the Central Council and the matter was then referred back to the Leinster Council. The Leinster Council, who were obviously aware that this was about to happen, had a meeting fixed for that Saturday evening.

A short few hours after this directive from the Central Council, the Leinster Council convened in Portlaoise, upheld the referee's report and confirmed that Offaly would play Wexford in the semi final. But this story was far from finished and the meeting rooms would be busy in the coming days with efforts to try and resolve a tricky situation.

The next stage resulted in Kildare taking their case to the CAC. While all this was going on, Wexford were still unsure who their semi final opponents would be.

In fact, with so much uncertainty surrounding the fixture, the date of the semi final was put back until July 2nd – the same date as the Leinster Hurling Final.

The CAC met on June 7th and heard the Kildare appeal. Their deliberations took approximately 30 minutes and it ruled in favour of the Leinster Council's decision to award the game to Offaly. That should have ended the matter, but this saga had one more hurdle to jump before it was brought to a conclusion.

It was another week before the DRA, which included former Dublin hero Kevin Heffernan, heard Kildare's appeal. This was Kildare's third appeal on the same issue, an unprecedented event in GAA history.

The hearing was scheduled for Thursday June 15th, and within hours of that meeting the DRA released its findings. Once again it was in Offaly's favour. Finally they could now concentrate on the upcoming Leinster semi final.

Kildare accepted the decision and their Chairman Sly Merrins said, 'we are disappointed to lose our case but we still believe that the blood substitution rule is open to serious abuse in its current form'.

Merrins continued, 'it is our

Dermot Earley, Kildare, rises highest against Neville Coughlan, left, and Ciaran McManus, Offaly to punch the ball clear. Kildare v Offaly, Leinster Football Quarter Final, Croke Park, Dublin. 28 May 2006

intention to bring a motion to Congress next year to address this situation but for now we will concentrate all our energies on our qualifier with Cavan in Newbridge next week. We hope we can achieve success and we wish our friends in Offaly all the best in their championship semi final.'

So a saga that began on the field in Croke Park on Sunday May 28th finally came to an end in the committee room also in Croke Park on June 15th, and all involved breathed a huge sigh of relief.

Could the entire saga have been avoided? Possibly, but the blood rule is so complicated even the most seasoned of GAA officials have been baffled by the wording. In fact, the rule fails to specify what exactly the status of the original blood substitute (James Coughlan in this case) was when he returned to the field after half-time.

One simple way out of the problem would have been to hand the fourth official two separate slips of paper: one with Kellaghan replacing Coughlan and the second one with Coughlan then replacing Trevor Phelan. Confusing, isn't it? You bet – the

football is far easier to report on!

When the dust settled and the games got underway again, Offaly made it to the Leinster final on a day when Wexford's Mattie Forde made headlines for all the wrong reasons and in the process landed the Leinster Council with another problem.

Kildare beat Cavan in the first round of the qualifiers, but were easily beaten by Derry in the next round.

As for the 'blood rule', it's still out there awaiting another victim.

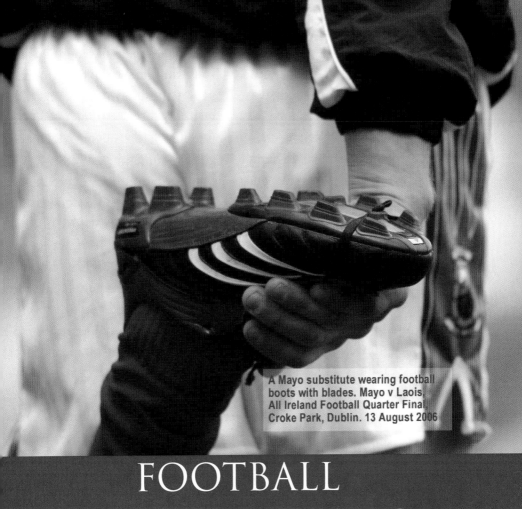

A Mayo substitute wearing football boots with blades. Mayo v Laois, All Ireland Football Quarter Final, Croke Park, Dublin. 13 August 2006

FOOTBALL QUARTER FINALS

AND NOW THERE ARE FOUR

It really was hotting up now. The race to succeed Tyrone as All Ireland football champions had intensified.

The first of the quarter finals took place on the August Bank Holiday Saturday, with Ulster v Munster pairings in both. A week later the men from the east and the west would engage in battle, with Dublin's unique drawing power giving them a stand alone fixture against Westmeath.

Kerry v Armagh

It was billed as the curtain raiser but it served as the main course as Kerry and Armagh produced a classic contest.

Kerry once again placed Kieran Donaghy at full-forward and adopted route one tactics. Kick it in high and let Donaghy do the rest. This time though the youngster from Tralee was being marked by wily old campaigner Francie Bellew. They had a ding-dong battle.

Armagh made the more positive start despite conceding an early goal to Eoin Brosnan. The sides were level on 21 minutes, when 2 minutes later Steven McDonnell got an Armagh goal, but it was 10 minutes before they scored again. Kerry with Dara O'Sé dominating midfield were growing in confidence and it showed.

In the closing minutes before the break they scored two points, which could easily have been goals. It meant for all their effort Armagh only led 1-7 to 1-5 at half-time.

The momentum was now with Kerry and they were a different team on the resumption.

Early points were followed by a spectacular goal from Donaghy, now getting the

Darren O'Sullivan, Kerry, intercepts a poor pass and drilled a powerful shot to the net. Armagh v Kerry, All Ireland Football Quarter Final, Croke Park, Dublin. 5 August 2006 better of Bellew. The O'Sé brothers Marc and Tomas between them bagged three points, Armagh were struggling as Kerry led 2-10 to 1-8. Joe Kernan rang the changes and his side responded with four of the next five points. It was now a two point game, Kerry 2-11 Armagh 1-12.

There followed an unsavoury incident, when Kerry's Paul Galvin already on a yellow card, foolishly got involved with an Armagh water carrier and for his troubles was sent off by referee Dave Coldrick. It could have been a difficult last ten minutes for Kerry, but a proud footballing county responded in style. They were helped by a dreadful error by corner-back Enda McNulty, whose poor hand pass sealed their fate.

Darren O'Sullivan intercepted and drilled a powerful shot to the net. Game over.

In the closing minutes Kerry tacked on a few more points as once again Armagh's championship ambitions lay in ruins and with it their dreams of a second title.

Kerry are back on track and such was the manner of their victory they are immediately installed as favourites to lift 'Sam'.

Cork v Donegal

It was always going to be a hard act to follow given what went before and for the opening 35 minutes Cork and Donegal struggled. The fact that a fair portion of the attendance (51,673), had departed may have been a contributory factor, but watching Kerry folk would have enjoyed a wry smile.

Donegal made a bright start and were boosted when Christy Toye punched home a fourth minute goal, the first Cork conceded in the Championship. Nicholas Murphy was to emerge as the key player as the contest evolved. In the 11th minute he won a penalty which John Hayes converted for Cork's first score.

It was, however, Donegal who showed the better form, spoiled though by some dreadful misses, that ultimately came back to haunt them. On 30 minutes it was 1-5 to 1-1 for the men from Tir Conaill in this first ever Championship meeting between the counties. But just as Kerry did in the opening game, Cork finished the half with two points, from James Masters and Fintan Goold. The margin was only 1-5 to 1-3 in Donegal's favour at the break.

The fare improved considerably in the second half, as Cork raised their level of performance and Donegal responded. Ger Spillane, Pierce O'Neill, Masters and Donnacha O'Connor all had points to edge Cork ahead.

Donegal came again and similar scores from Brendan Boyle, Michael Doherty and Colin Kelly restored their lead briefly. They extended it to two points when Ciaran Bonner and Kevin McMahon traded points. The initiative was now firmly with Cork, principally because Murphy was controlling midfield. The fitness of Billy Morgan's men was also a factor.

Masters and Sean O'Brien brought them level and as injury time beckoned a replay looked certain. However, there was to be a dramatic finale. Murphy fetched one from the clouds and fed Spillane who drilled the leather between the sticks. Cork in front 1-11 to 1-10. Back came Donegal and Bonner's mighty effort looked destined to force a second meeting, but it fell into the arms of Alan Quirke and seconds later a shrill blast of referee Thomas Quigley's whistle signalled the end. Not only of Donegal's

challenge but also that of Ulster's as for the first time in the history of the Championship, the province would not be represented in the last four.

Dublin v Westmeath

The start may have been put back by fifteen minutes to allow the Dublin supporters into the ground, annoying for the opposition when there is no travel involved, but it only delayed the inevitable as Westmeath were outclassed. Ciaran Whelan was immense in the middle of the field, while in attack Jason Sherlock showed flashes of the old Jayo as he teased and tormented the opposition defence. In the opening twenty-five minutes he was instrumental in either setting up or scoring six of their first seven points. In the same period they also squandered two clear goal chances that on another day they could rue.

The only goal of a poor contest arrived somewhat fortuitously in the 13th minute, when Tomas Quinn reacted quickest to a ball that came back off the upright to drill it to the net from an acute angle. Even at this stage the contest was in danger of dying on its feet. By half-time it needed life

Jason Sherlock, Dublin, prevents Donal O'Donoghue, Westmeath from getting possession. All Ireland Football Quarter Final, Dublin v Westmeath, Croke Park, Dublin. 12 August 2006

support. Dublin were 1-7 to 0-2 in front and Westmeath were clearly in for a torrid afternoon. The second half struggled to take on any discernible shape, not helped by Dublin's wastefulness in front of goal and the weakness of Westmeath's challenge. There was a long period when neither side could buy a score. Westmeath went 27 minutes without scoring until Michael Ennis notched a point. The game petered out and long before the end Dublin's place in the semi final was secure. However, they were still unsure about the actual merit of their challenge. Nonetheless, their drawing power was never more evident as 79,100 watched them become convincing winners by 1-12 to 0-5. There were few complaints from the hordes on the Hill.

Mayo v Laois

It looked very much like the same old story, time ebbing away and Mayo trailing Laois by two points. Another tale of woe for the men from the West, or so it seemed. But Mickey Moran maintains that this is a different breed of footballer wearing the 'red and green', and they proved him right. With yet another Croke Park defeat staring them in the face, they battled back.

It was an absorbing contest from the off, devoid of cynicism, off the ball squabbles or verbal spats. It was just pure football – a rarity in the Championship up to now.

Mayo got the opening two points, but quickly found themselves four points in arrears as Ross Munnelly, Chris Conway and Noel Garvan each scored two points. It took Mayo until the 23rd minute to register another point, and they soon battled back as the pendulum swung in their direction. Ciarán McDonald was once again orchestrating the fight back.

Indeed Mayo ripped the Laois defence apart on a number of occasions. With a bit more composure in front of goal Mayo could have scored two if not three goals. As it was they were just a point behind at half-time, 0-8 to 0-7 for the men from the O'Moore County.

Five minutes into the second half, Mayo, courtesy of two Mortimer points, were in front. Then enter Donie Brennan.

The diminutive but highly talented star knocked over two points. Laois ahead again and only a timely block by Aidan Higgins denied Munnelly a certain Laois goal.

However this invigorating contest had a few more twists in it.

It ebbed and flowed as Mayo once again regained the lead in the 58th minute, but six minutes later Laois had kicked three unanswered points to retake the lead by two points. A date with the Dubs was looming large on the horizon, strengthened when a mighty leap by Noel Garvan plucked McDonald's long range effort from under the crossbar.

Mayo though were not to be denied and they battled back from the abyss. Aidan Kilcoyne kicked a splendid point. Then in the last act of a quality game, Conor Mortimer pointed a free to ensure a second day out that was thoroughly deserved.

Ciarán McDonald, Mayo, fields a high ball against Billy Sheehan, Laois. Mayo v Laois, All Ireland Football Quarter Final, Croke Park, Dublin. 13 August 2006

Mayo make no mistake

And so to the replay. It looked ominous for Laois early on when the normally reliable Ross Munnelly missed an easy free that would have given them the lead. As it was, Billy Joe Padden and

Ger Brady scored Mayo points, who at one stage led by 0-7 to 0-2. Laois did get late points to give them some hope for the second half.

Despite playing poorly, Laois reduced the deficit to two points

0-10 to 0-8 by the 53rd minute. However, three unanswered points eased Mayo into a commanding lead of 0-13 to 0-8.

Laois rallied again but the goal they needed never came and it is Mayo who were heading back to Croke Park a week later for a tilt at a Dublin side, untested to date in the Championship.

It may have lacked the quality of the drawn encounter but that will not trouble Mickey Moran's Mayo.

Defeat for Laois also, for now at least, signalled the end of Mick O'Dwyer's managerial career with the O'Moore County side.

O'Dwyer, 70 years of age, had few complaints after a poor performance saying, 'I suppose the number of big games we had to play in successive weeks eventually took its toll as we were very leaden footed out there today, but we had a good run and a credit to Mayo they deserved the win'.

So Mayo march on to face the Dubs! Could Dublin pass this test or would Mayo upset all the odds and reach yet another All Ireland final?

For many the possibility of the so called dream final was inching ever nearer, but Mayo were still very much in the equation.

Cork and Waterford players stand for the National Anthem. Cork v Waterford. All Ireland Hurling Semi Final, Croke Park, Dublin. 6 August 2006

HURLING SEMI FINALS

The Hurling Championship 2006 finally got the boost it badly needed as 62,000 supporters watched two sparkling semi finals –
Cork v Waterford *and* ***Kilkenny v Clare****.*

Cork v Waterford

It badly needed a lift and it got it. The Guinness All Ireland Hurling Championship finally sparked on a gloomy August afternoon in Croke Park. Close on 62,000 supporters watched as Cork were pitted against Waterford in the first semi final.

It was a meeting that had captured the imagination of supporters from both counties, as Waterford sought to reach their first final since 1963. Cork on the other hand were bidding to make it to their fourth successive decider. Contrasting form in the quarter finals had seen Waterford installed as favourites. Was the Cork tank running on empty or had the men from the 'Decies' timed their run to perfection?

Waterford were without the injured Dave Bennett and also decided against starting team captain Paul Flynn as he too was carrying an injury. It would later emerge that the Ballygunner star felt fit enough to start and was disappointed at not being included.

Cork's early form would suggest that they had plenty in the tank, as they opened up a 0-4 to 0-2 lead, with Brian Corcoran scoring two sublime points. Crucially their defence was containing the threat from the Waterford attack. Sean Óg kept a tight rein on Dan Shanahan, Brian Murphy held John Mullane, while Ronan Curran was dominant at centre-back.

Eoin Kelly and Ken McGrath were keeping Waterford in touch with their free taking. In fact it took Waterford 34 minutes to score from play, and that came after a rare mistake from Ó'hAilpín

which allowed Shanahan in for hi only score of the match.

Another important aspect of th contest was the outstandin display of Cork goalkeeper Dona Óg Cusack, who despite th greasy conditions, handled th ball impeccably and inspired thos around him.

Shanahan's point lifted th Waterford challenge and Mullan slipped over two points to brin the sides level at the break 0- apiece. As the sides left the field was the Waterford supporters wh appeared the happier. Could the end their long wait for a fin appearance? Many felt they wou never get a better chance.

This view was reinforced withi 60 seconds of the restart, when Eoin Kelly knocked in a goal, but only after Cusack had twice denied Eoin McGrath.

Seamus Prendergast added a point and now it was 1-9 to 0-8 for Waterford. Was the long famine about to end? Cork though had other ideas.

Cork don't 'do panic' and they raised the tempo of their game as the stadium throbbed with excitement. The champion: scored three of the next fou points from Niall Ronan, Timm

McCarthy and Gerry O'Connor. Eoin Kelly pointed a free and now it was 1-11 to 0-11 for Waterford. But the initiative was with Cork as they slowly tightened their grip and swung the semi final in their direction. Defensively they had retained control. Waterford went 17 minutes without a score. Then just as he had done in last year's semi final, Cork boss John Allen played his trump card. 19 year-old Cathal Naughton was sprung from the bench.

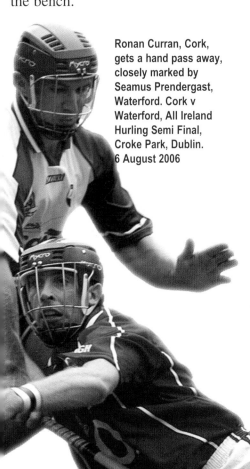

Ronan Curran, Cork, gets a hand pass away, closely marked by Seamus Prendergast, Waterford. Cork v Waterford, All Ireland Hurling Semi Final, Croke Park, Dublin. 6 August 2006

It was to prove an inspired substitution and it ripped the heart out of the Waterford challenge.

In the 57th minute with his first touch, he hit a superb point. Two minutes later after taking a pass from Deane, Naughton belied his lack of big match experience to fire in a classic goal, and as the raindrops fell from the net at the Canal end of the ground, it was to be the game's defining moment. Gerry O'Connor hit another spectacular point and the tide had turned, Cork 1-14 to 1-11 in front.

Waterford were stunned. Eoin Kelly pointed a badly-needed free, immediately cancelled out by Deane for Cork. The tension was palpable as Waterford, who by now had introduced Flynn, cut the deficit to a point as the 70th minute approached.

Deane from a difficult angle put two between the sides again. Mullane replied for Waterford. Heading for injury time and with just one point separating two heroic sides.

One last twist. Waterford win a free on their own '65'. Up stepped Ken McGrath and whether it was an O'Neill's or an All-Star sliotar he had to score to force a replay. As the ball flew through the mist-shrouded sky it seemed destined to reach its target, but Cusack diverted it away and seconds later the full time whistle sounded. Cork by a point, 1-16 to 1-15.

There were mixed scenes of emotion around the ground. Unbridled joy for the 'Rebels' as the players saluted their fans, while for those loyal and dedicated Waterford supporters, heartbreak yet again.

Cork defied the critics and are now on the brink of history. Only Clare or Kilkenny stand between them and the three-in-a-row.

Semi Final
Cork **1-16**
Waterford **1-15**

Kilkenny v Clare

There was a dramatic start. Within 60 seconds Henry Shefflin, after a mistake by the normally reliable Brian Lohan, drilled a powerful shot past Davy Fitzgerald for a Kilkenny goal. The rangy Ballyhale Shamrock's man then added two points and it looked ominous for Clare. However, there is immense pride in Anthony Daly's men and with veteran

Seanie McMahon leading the charge they battled back. Kilkenny's full-back line was in all sorts of trouble and paid the price in the seventh minute when Niall Gilligan poked home a goal. It gave the Banner County renewed confidence. Unfortunately for them they spurned three clear goal chances at a time when Kilkenny were vulnerable. That ultimately undid their challenge.

The first half saw the sides trade some quality points. McMahon and Shefflin in particular were unerring in their shooting. Clare went in front, briefly, and with the game now being played at a relentless pace the worry was would the long-serving men from the Banner stay the distance?

Such was the closeness of the scoring it came as no real surprise that it was all square 1-10 each at half-time.

Kilkenny had lost John Tennyson with a shoulder injury. While Shefflin rarely missed, his forward colleagues were not as accurate and they accumulated 11 wides, 20 in total over the 70 minutes.

Kilkenny reshaped their defence for the second half with Tommy

Martin Comerford, Kilkenny, in a duel to win possession with Brian Lohan, Clare. Kilkenny v Clare, All Ireland Hurling Semi Final, Croke Park, Dublin. 13 August 2006

Walsh reverting to his more natural corner-back position. As a consequence there was a steadier look to the Cats' rearguard. This is reflected in the fact that Clare only scored six points in that second half, and yet their incredible battling qualities kept them in contention.

Clare though were finding the going tough and trailed by two points, 1-14 to 1-12, when Kilkenny struck for their second goal, courtesy of substitute Eoin McCormack. To their credit, Clare got the next four points to reduce the deficit to a point, but the normally reliable Niall Gilligan missed a relatively easy free. It signalled the end of their challenge.

Kilkenny by now had switched

Shefflin onto McMahon and it worked a treat, as Shefflin's pace and strength wore down the Doora-Barefield man and the match-clinching points quickly followed.

Shefflin himself knocked over a few, bringing his tally in a man of the match performance to 1-13, as did Cha Fitzpatrick who also impressed in midfield.

His youthful exuberance proving too good for long-serving Colin Lynch. Clare's cause was not helped by the dismissal of Frank Lohan, who along with McMahon was outstanding. But by then, the game had slipped from their grasp and Kilkenny's place in the final was secure on a 2-21 to 1-16 scoreline.

For 65 minutes it was nip and tuck before a late scoring burst by

Diarmuid McMahon, Clare, on a determined solo run. Kilkenny v Clare, All Ireland Hurling Semi Final, Croke Park, Dublin. 13 August 2006

Kilkenny ended Clare's brave resistance and probably the careers of some of the county's most accomplished hurlers. Brian Lohan was the first to go a few short weeks after this match. Manager Anthony Daly also signalled that he too would depart, 'I said this would be my last year and I intend sticking by that decision.'

It meant that for the third time in four years Cork and Kilkenny would contest the Guinness All Ireland Hurling Final, and already the mind games were beginning. Kilkenny boss Brian Cody said, 'Cork will be favourites and right now we are just delighted to be in the final, after a tough battle from a great Clare team'.

The last time these great rivals met in a final, Cork denied Kilkenny a much sought after three-in-a-row. Now it's the Rebels who are seeking a three-in-a-row. with the Cats determined to deny them.

The scramble for tickets was underway as the hurling season draws to a close, while a nation waits in expectation of a classic.

Semi Final
Kilkenny 2-21
Clare 1-16

The Laois manager Mick O'Dwyer enters the Laois dressing room in Croke Park. Laois v Mayo, All Ireland Football Quarter Final Replay, Croke Park, Dublin. 20 August 2006

MANAGERIAL CASUALTIES

A number of high profile GAA managers lost their jobs in 2006 – a few left on their own terms.

It is said that the only certainty about being a manager is that you end up getting sacked. Yes, it even happens in the GAA. Some though go on their own terms. Others outstay their welcome and are often moved aside by an uneasy county board.

First to Go

The first manager to vacate or to be sacked from his position in 2006 was Dominic Corrigan, the Fermanagh man who was the Sligo football boss.

The previous year Corrigan, who is a highly respected coach, had done a reasonable job with the Yeats County and was looking forward to a good league campaign. However, successive defeats proved too much for the county board. The fact that the losses came at the hands of Waterford and Tipperary, two counties that Sligo would have expected to beat, did not help.

It was a wet Tuesday evening in February and Corrigan was on the field organising a training session. Then a van drew up and from it alighted two county board officials, including the Chairman, who informed him that his services were no longer required.

Corrigan was furious. Having spent the day teaching in St Michael's College, Enniskillen, he had then driven to Sligo, where he was in effect sacked from his position as senior football manager.

It might have been easier to pick up the phone and tell Corrigan that his time was up. At least he would not have had to endure the long journey home contemplating his future.

The Chairman did say, 'they owed it to Dominic to tell him to

Dominic Corrigan, Sligo manager, was the first manager to lose his job in 2006. Successive defeats proved too much for the Sligo County Board. Cork v Sligo, Football qualifiers, Round 4. O'Moore Park, Portlaoise, Co. Laois. 30 July 2005

his face that his contract was been terminated'.

As usual there was a brief outcry from some officials within the county, but the officers rode out the storm, appointed former player Tommy Breheny in his place and moved on. Sligo finished mid-table in Division 2 of the National League, exited the

Connacht championship at the hands of Roscommon, but had a surprise yet deserved win over Down in the qualifiers.

Crossley walks in Down

Down were the next county to go shopping for a manager, this time in hurling, as dissatisfaction with John Crossley's reign surfaced in the Mourne County.

Competing in Division 1 of the league was always going to be tough and a series of heavy defeats did little for morale. Crossley had enlisted the help of Seanie Farrell from Cork. It is possible that his presence may have undermined the manager, although Farrell is on record as saying he never sought the position.

Results and relations worsened and soon Crossley decided enough was enough and resigned. Seanie Farrell was appointed in his place. He kept them in Division 1 of the league. However, a surprise defeat to Carlow in the Christy Ring Cup saw Farrell walk, leaving Down seeking a third hurling manager in one season.

Garden County lose Kenny

The first casualty of the Championship was Hugh Kenny of Wicklow. It was his last season anyway, but when the Garden County lost to Carlow in the Leinster Football Championship, Hugh was on his way.

Kenny felt that as he would not be involved in 2007 it would be preferable if a new man took charge for the qualifiers. It made little difference as Wicklow's season ended when they lost to Monaghan.

Ennis defeat ends McKenna's reign

Limerick hurling has been in the headlines over the last few seasons – mostly for all the wrong reasons. However, a good league campaign under Joe McKenna appeared to have steadied the ship. Playing a nice brand of hurling, Limerick had reached the final, where they gave a good account of themselves before losing to Kilkenny. No shame in that and they faced into the Championship in confident mood.

Tipperary were their first round opponents and based on league form, McKenna's men were favourites to win. But that afternoon in Thurles it all began to unravel.

Tipperary won a poor game, and once again Limerick headed for the qualifiers, and with it more turmoil.

Strangely enough, they seemed to have recovered well from the Championship defeat and reports indicated they had an excellent training session four days after that game.

However, at the conclusion of this session a member of the management team berated the players for not, in his words, 'adhering to the game plan against Tipperary'. Some players asked the question 'what game plan?'

Undercurrents within the squad suggested yet another 'them and us' situation was fast developing.

There were two other significant developments that effectively signalled the end of McKenna's reign.

The first was a challenge game against a weakened Galway team. Limerick won, but it was far from impressive. Sloppy Galway defending saw them concede three goals which did not give a true picture of the depth of problems Limerick had.

Then a week before they played Clare in Ennis, a bonding weekend was held at the Heritage Hotel in Portlaoise. During the course of that weekend the players had a meeting and the dominant theme was that the training wasn't sufficiently intense.

It was clear then that all was not well. Indeed privately some players

Limerick manager Joe McKenna pictured at the Galway v Limerick game. Allianz National Hurling League, Division 1B, Round 2, Pearse Stadium, Galway. 26 February 2006

Derry manager Paddy Crozier at the Donegal v Derry game. Ulster Football Semi Final, St. Tighearnach's Park, Clones, Co. Monaghan. 18 June 2006

was announced. A raft of changes all contributed to a dreadful first half performance.

The entire deck of cards collapsed at half-time in the dressing room. Words were exchanged between a number of players and the coach. As a result of this, even though it may be denied, goalkeeper Brian Murray was replaced and with division rife, the game both on and off the field was up.

Clare ran riot in the second half, scored 11 points without reply at one stage, and Limerick's only point from play came five minutes from time.

By 6.30pm that evening, McKenna and team coach Ger Cunningham had tendered their resignations. Trainer Dave Maheady followed a few days later. In fact it was left to TJ Ryan to inform the players of these events, as McKenna or Cunningham did not attend the team meal after the game.

So yet again Limerick hurling was embroiled in another crisis. It was left to former stars Richie Bennis and Gary Kirby to pick up the pieces, while the players' response was being watched with interest.

anticipated the capitulation that followed in Ennis. The management obviously did not. There were reports also that one player who impressed during the league indulged in three heavy drinking sessions after the Championship loss to Tipperary.

Team morale was further dented when the starting 15 for the match

To be fair it was positive and a thumping win over Offaly put them back in contention for a quarter final place in the All Ireland. They only lost to Cork by one point after a titanic battle.

Brief spat in Derry

Derry football manager Paddy Crozier and his selectors resigned and returned within the space of seven days in a dispute with the county board. It all stemmed from a refusal by the board's Games Administration Committee (GAC) to postpone a series of club league games involving members of the county squad.

When contacted about his resignation, Crozier denied he had stepped down, and apparently told the BBC that it must be the Derry hurling manager Sean McCloskey who had resigned.

Derry were due to play Dublin in a challenge match on Saturday morning, but on hearing of the manager's situation the players refused to travel and the game was called off. It is understood the management were prepared to play but senior members of the squad were reluctant to play two games in the space of 24 hours. The contentious round of league

games went ahead as scheduled.

Talks at bringing about a resolution got underway immediately. However, little progress was made before they adjourned as the officials of the board were due to attend a county final.

Ulster Council officials were reported to have agreed to act as mediators, but the Derry board suffered a financial loss.

Along with the challenge game being postponed, so too was a 'bonding weekend' in the National Sports Institute in Limerick, leaving the board out of pocket, as deposits for the stay were paid in advance.

With the players rowing in behind Crozier, they immediately withdrew their services to the county team. The county board knew they had to resolve the matter quickly, especially as an Ulster championship game with Tyrone was coming up in a couple of weeks.

Three days of exhaustive talks solved the problem as the management, players and the county board officials thrashed out a compromise. Both parties were happy with the outcome but refused to reveal details of the settlement.

It was understood that county league games were brought forward by 24 hours to facilitate the senior panel. The players who had withdrawn their services in support of Crozier returned to training and a line was drawn under the entire incident.

A united front was presented at the launch of the Ulster championship and it did Derry little harm as they beat Tyrone in the first round to send the All Ireland champions to the qualifiers, again.

The Departures continue

As the season evolved and teams exited the Championship, the fate of many managers was decided. Liam Hayes stepped down as Carlow football boss, followed by Martin McElkennon in Cavan. McElkennon has since joined the Monaghan backroom team as trainer.

Paddy O'Rourke's four year reign as Down boss was also brought to an end by the county board, despite the fact that O'Rourke – a former All Ireland winner – was keen to remain in charge.

County chairman Jerry Quinn was a known supporter of O'Rourke, but following the loss to Sligo in the qualifiers in which they scored just 0-4, the mood in the county was for change. A lengthy board meeting decided the manager's fate. The decision did not sit well with the senior players who held O'Rourke in high esteem.

They issued a statement expressing their disappointment at the decision as did O'Rourke who had invested a lot of time in the job, but the die was cast. Down would have a new man at the helm for 2007 as they bid to regain former glories in a province where they were once the kingpins.

Laois hurling boss Dinny Cahill also had his services dispensed with following a season in which the county won just one game all year. The Tipperary native who had enjoyed a good innings with Antrim, winning three Ulster titles, came with excellent credentials, but left with a record that made for depressing reading. There was rumours too, substantiated in most cases, of a squad disillusioned and divided. Laois were relegated from Division 1 of the league and only preserved their status as a Tier 1 hurling county by defeating Westmeath in the last game of the season. It was also Cahill's final outing as boss.

Clare hurling boss Anthony Daly completed his third and final year at the helm after the semi final loss to Kilkenny. Seamus Murphy's departure in Wexford came as no surprise really given the paucity of their challenge in the All Ireland quarter final defeat by Clare.

Conor Hayes did not seek another year in charge of the Galway hurlers and rumours were rife that former Clare supremo Ger Loughnane was about to return to inter-county management.

He initially denied he was interested in the job to Diarmuid Flynn of the *Irish Examiner*. However, 48 hours later, writing in his column in *The Daily Star*, Loughnane confirmed that he had agreed to be nominated for the position.

There were five other candidates nominated: Clare goalkeeper Davy Fitzgerald, former Galway star Sean Silke, former manager Mattie Murphy, Portumna boss Sean Treacy and former Clare star Pat O'Connor.

There was a groundswell of support for Loughnane – the senior hurling panel issuing a statement backing his appointment although it emerged later that some players were not consulted on this statement.

O'Connor, Fitzgerald and Treacy withdrew from the race, but Silke and Murphy did not. A further development saw former referee Jimmy Cooney, who was involved in the controversial All Ireland semi final between Clare and Offaly in 1998, come out in support of Loughnane. In a direct response to that statement, former Galway hurling star, Joe Cooney, Jimmy's brother spoke out against Loughnane's appointment. This move surprised many people given Joe's quiet disposition and unwillingness to be part of such a public debate.

Then in another startling development, Loughnane issued a statement saying 'he was withdrawing from the race, as he did not want to get involved in a contest'. The county was stunned at this, especially in view of the support Loughnane now enjoyed. Indeed at a Hurling Board meeting 30 of 35 speakers expressed the view that Loughnane's appointment would benefit the game in Galway.

Behind the scenes, the county board officers swung into action in an effort to resolve the matter.

Murphy and Silke subsequently issued statements announcing their withdrawal from the race, but Murphy made it clear he was not supporting any other nominee. Silke immediately backed Loughnane.

Loughnane now had a clear run and indicated he was willing to rethink his position. A scheduled meeting of the Galway hurling board was cancelled. This was done, in the opinion of some observers, to give Loughnane an opportunity to put his backroom team in place.

With no opposition, Ger Loughnane, the man who brought the Liam McCarthy Cup to Clare in 1995 and 1997, has become Limerick hurling manager and will be patrolling the sidelines during the Championship of 2007, this time with Galway.

O'Dwyer departs in Laois

70-year-old Mick O'Dwyer left Croke Park on August 20th having seen his Laois side lose to Mayo in the All Ireland quarter final replay, adamant he would not return. O'Dwyer had stated early in the year that this would be his last with the county. Now the ink had barely dried on the following days' newspapers when efforts were underway to get the genial Waterville maestro to remain at the helm. All efforts failed and O'Dwyer's leaving of Laois was officially confirmed by the county board on September 6th.

The man who had led Kerry in a golden era and also took Kildare to a Leinster title is keen to stay in football, but not with Laois. The question now was which county would benefit from his vast experience, and as they say 'hold the back page'.

Former Limerick manager and Kerry native Liam Kearns has been appointed to succeed Mick O'Dwyer's footsteps and become Laois football manager. Kearns could be joined by Sean Dempsey who enjoyed a successful spell with the O'Moore County's minor and under 21 team.

Barry's tenure terminated

It ended as it began – in controversy. If Sean Boylan was the longest serving manager in Meath's football history, then Eamonn Barry's reign will go down as the shortest.

His appointment in November of last year (2005) may very well have had the backing of the majority of clubs in the county, but it did not sit well with a number of officials. Indeed there is a widely held view that the manner in which his initial appointment was handled could have cost Fintan McGinnity his position as county Chairman, a post he occupied for over thirty years.

In previous years the clubs would nominate and then vote in the manager of the senior football. Crucially that process was changed this year (2006), and more power was given to the officers, who in turn appointed a sub-committee to oversee the process. That effectively sealed Barry's fate. In fact Barry himself said he was aware as far back as May that he would not be reappointed.

The problems date back to Barry's time as manager of the Meath junior football team and an incident in the dressing room before an All Ireland final against Kerry. Ever since Barry and officialdom have been on different wavelengths.

Despite the fact that he felt he would not be reappointed, Barry proceeded to hold a players' meeting on Monday 4th September 2006. This annoyed the County Board officers, who wanted the meeting cancelled. In their efforts to get the meeting deferred, the Board officers sent a letter, hand delivered by the secretary's wife at 4 pm to Barry's house. However, Barry was unaware of the letter until he arrived home that night at 10pm after the meeting had taken place in Walterstown.

The county board meeting to ratify Colm Coyle as manager of the senior football team was held on September 11th and the proposal by Chairman Brendan Dempsey took many delegates by surprise.

A lengthy debate followed, with some members asking that the matter be referred back to their clubs for further consideration.

One club delegate went so far as to say that 'the county board are trying to shaft one management team and bulldoze another one on to us'.

Amendments were proposed, accepted and withdrawn as the debate dragged on. Eventually, amid confusion, the recommendation of the top table was passed. This was despite the fact that no official count was taken, only a show of hands from delegates (some voted others did not) before Dempsey declared Colm Coyle the new manager.

When the news broke, Barry was very critical of the process that saw him removed after just one season, claiming that three of the men central to Coyle's appointment had voted against him last year, a claim refuted by Chairman Dempsey.

'Eamonn was given a fair crack of the whip – just like all other candidates, and there is no way of knowing who voted for or against him last year. We followed due process at our meeting in what was a new appointment process in Meath. I would like to thank Eamonn and his backroom team for all the work they put in this year.'

So after twenty-three years of Sean Boylan, Meath will start 2007 with their third manager in three years. Colm Coyle will have Tommy Dowd and Dudley Farrell, as his selectors. Their progress will be watched with interest.

Elsewhere

Kevin Kilmurray departed his job as the Offaly football manager following two years at the helm. He would have been offered a further term but decided it was time to move on.

Tipperary football boss Seamus McCarthy who has given a lifetime of service to the game in the Premier county also stepped down after two years, during which they won the Tommy Murphy Cup. McCarthy, a bank official based in Cork, cited business commitments as his reason for leaving. Former star Johnny Owens, a selector with McCarthy, was named as his successor.

In Limerick, Ritchie Bennis who took temporary control following Joe McKenna's resignation in June, was given the position of senior hurling manager on a permanent basis. Included in his backroom team are his nephew Gary Kirby and former star Bernie Hartigan, as they begin a two year term.

Cork hurling boss John Allen decided not to seek a third year at the helm of the Rebels saying, 'it's time for a change, it's been a fabulous few years and to be involved in so many outstanding games with a great group was a real privilege'.

John guided Cork to the All Ireland title in his first year in charge, saw his side embark on a twelve match unbeaten run in the Championship, won back-to-back Munster titles and came very close to winning the three-in-a-row.

THE BEST
OF THE REST

*GAA sports also
include Camogie,
Ladies' Football,
Colleges'
competitions,
Minor, Junior and
Intermediate
competitions,
Handball and Puc
Fada competitions.*

For many supporters the GAA season begins and ends with the All Ireland Hurling and Football Championships in September, but that only tells part of the story. It has now become to all intents and purposes a twelve-month season. Such a scenario may not appeal to everyone. The genuine GAA supporter, of which there are thousands the length and breadth of the country, will watch their team in all sorts of weather.

Colleges and third-level institutions in both codes and in camogie and ladies' football have also expanded their competitions.

Croke Park opened its doors for the first time in February when the Junior and Intermediate Club Hurling Finals were held. It was to prove a historic occasion as Cork side Fr O'Neill's captured the Junior title, while Dicksboro from Kilkenny were crowned intermediate champions.

A week later it was the turn of the footballers. In Junior, the honours went to Ardfert from Kerry, who had Sinn Féin TD Martin Ferris as a selector. The Intermediate title was won by Monaghan side, Inniskeen.

Third-level competitions are now highly rated and much sought after with many of the country's top players taking part in these exciting championships. The fact that they are very often played in the worst of the weather in no way lessens their appeal.

In the Datapac Sigerson Cup, Dublin City University were hosting the competition for the first time. They ended as winners under the lights of Parnell Park on a cold February night.

In hurling, the Fitzgibbon Cup is one of the oldest cups in the GAA. Waterford Institute of Technology may be relative newcomers to the competition, but they won their eighth title with ease, defeating UCD in a one-sided final.

In camogie, University of Limerick took the prestigious Ashbourne Cup, while at national level the league title was won by Cork who defeated Tipperary in the final in Thurles.

Kilkenny once dominated the senior championship but in recent years they have been out of the honours. However, by winning the newly inaugurated under 16 All Ireland championship they could be giving a sign that they are on the way back.

In Ladies' Football, Cork retained the Suzuki Division 1 National League, a title they collected for the first time in 2005.

Dublin Colleges gave hurling in the capital a huge boost with a great win over famed St Flannan's of Ennis to take the All Ireland Colleges' title. In football, it took extra time before Abbey CBS from Newry defeated St Pat's from Navan in a thriller before a big crowd in Dr Cullen Park, Carlow.

In Vocational Schools, St Brogan's from Bandon in County Cork suffered the heartbreak of losing both the hurling and football finals. St Fergal's from

A dejected Brian O'Sullivan, Ballinhassig, at the end of the game. All Ireland Club Intermediate Hurling Championship Final, Dicksboro v Ballinhassig, Croke Park, Dublin. 12 February 2006

Rathdowney in Laois won the hurling title, but the scenes of joy that greeted Virginia Colleges win in football were unmatched. It was the first ever title won by a Cavan college, an historic occasion in Nenagh.

Wicklow won the Vocational Inter-County Football title. Cork were winners of the hurling championship, beating Tipperary after a replay in the final.

The long established Puc Fada competition was once again held on the August Bank Holiday weekend over the Annaverna Mountains, Ravensdale in County Louth and it proved to be as entertaining as ever.

Conditions were difficult as one would expect with mist descending on the mountain, but this highly organised competition was run with meticulous planning by the committee and it went without a hitch. It is also dependent on the support of members of the local club, who steward the course, and it is generously sponsored by Martin Donnelly, a man with a passion for the GAA.

Tipperary goalkeeper Brendan Cummins covered the tough terrain in the least amount of shots and was duly crowned All Ireland Puc Fada champion for 2006.

The secondary competitions on the inter-county scene continued and while their appeal may be lessening, there is no doubting the commitment of the players who take great pride in wearing the county jersey.

Kerry captured the All Ireland Junior Football title, while in hurling, Cork, with a late burst in extra-time, defeated old rivals Kilkenny to win the Intermediate Championship, their fourth in six years.

There was a huge outpouring of emotion in Cusack Park, Ennis as Mayo beat Cork to capture the Cadbury's All Ireland Under 21 Football Championship.

Tipperary won the Hurling title with an easy win over Galway who were seeking three-in-a-row. In football Roscommon won the final replay against Kerry, thus ending a 55-year wait for the Tommy Markham Cup to return to the county, amid great scenes of jubilation.

Louth have not enjoyed the trappings of success since their one and only day in the sun back in 1957 when they defeated Cork in the All Ireland Football Final, but they will have happy memories of 2006.

In April they won Division 2 of the National Football League, while in August they returned to Croke Park and came away with the Tommy Murphy Cup following a comfortable win over Leitrim.

In camogie, Dublin for the second year in a row were crowned All Ireland Junior Champions, a sign perhaps that a revival of the county's fortunes may be on the way.

Handball is another sport with tangible links to the GAA. Croke Park houses a fabulous and ultra modern court and it has witnessed many a stirring contest. The big competition of the year was the World Handball Championships which took place in Edmonton, Canada and it featured an Irish double.

Fiona Shannon from St Paul's Club in Belfast won the Women's Open Single's title. In the final, Fiona, who played camogie for Antrim, defeated Anna Christoff from the USA 21-13, 21-11 with a fantastic display.

Paul Brady is an outstanding footballer with his native Cavan, but he showed his class with glove and ball to collect the Men's Open Single's title, with a 21-7, 21-11 win over Tony Healy from Cork, a feat in itself to have two Irish handballers contesting the final at such a world class championship.

Billy Morgan, the Cork manager, (serving a one-match touchline ban and forced to watch from the Stand) stands for the National Anthem. Kerry v Cork, All Ireland Football Semi Final, Croke Park, Dublin. 20 August 2006

FOOTBALL SEMI FINALS

*For the third time in the 2006 Championship, **Kerry** face arch rivals and Muster champions, **Cork**, while **Dublin** hope to dispose of the challenge of **Mayo**.*

Kerry v Cork

In their third meeting in the Bank of Ireland Championship 2006, Kerry faced arch rivals and Munster champions Cork seeking qualification for their third successive All Ireland final. Billy Morgan was forced to watch from the stands, serving a one-match touchline ban. The Munster champions were hoping to repeat their form of earlier rounds.

Cork were again without the injured Graham Canty, while Kerry's deployment of Kiera

Donaghy at full-forward caused endless problems for a beleaguered Rebel defence.

Kerry had shown remarkable improvement since the replay of the Munster final and were clear favourites entering this game. It was also their third meeting in five years at the semi final stage of the championship and the Kingdom had won the previous two encounters, with a bit to spare.

Croke Park was also a factor as Kerry teams invariably perform better when they leave the confines of Munster.

Kerry reacted to defeat in the Munster final by reshaping their defence to cope with the expected threat from the Cork attack, an acknowledgement that they were concerned.

Midfield was also going to be crucial as Nicholas Murphy had dominated the earlier clashes and Dara Ó'Sé was determined not to be outplayed again. There was an edge to the early exchanges, not unexpected given the familiarity that exists between these keen rivals.

Cork's Conor McCarthy opened the scoring with a nice point. Kerry were quickly on level terms when Sean O'Sullivan pointed a

Aidan O'Mahony, Kerry, fields a high ball ahead of Nicholas Murphy, Cork. Kerry v Cork, All Ireland Football Semi Final, Croke Park, Dublin. 20 August 2006

sideline kick, that ironically should have been awarded to Cork.

Further points from Donnacha O'Connor and James Masters edged Cork two points clear, but Kerry looked far more dangerous in attack. Donaghy was winning possession with ease, despite the best efforts of Cork full-back Derek Kavanagh. Indeed the big full-forward had legitimate claims for a penalty ignored. He was also twice denied goals by the brilliance of Cork goalkeeper Alan Quirke. O'Sé was also emerging as the game's central character, eclipsing Murphy in midfield, picking up a yellow card for his troubles on the way. Masters and Mike Frank Russell then traded points, but it was looking ominous for Cork.

Kerry moved up a gear with three points from Tomás O'Sé, Russell and O'Sullivan to take the lead, briefly cancelled out when Masters had Cork's fifth point in 12 minutes. However there was no stopping Kerry. Russell had his third point sandwiched in between two lovely pointed frees from Colm Cooper. These scores helped Kerry to an interval lead of 0-8 to 0-6. As the teams headed

for the dressing room there was already a feeling that Kerry had one foot in the decider.

Billy Morgan re-jigged his side for the second half and they did start promisingly. It took a timely intervention by the outstanding Seamus Moynihan to deny Cork a goal that would have re-ignited their challenge.

In fact a couple of times throughout the second half, Cork wasted opportunities that would have kept them closer to Kerry.

The sides each scored two points, but when Paul Galvin and Russell extended Kerry's advantage to five points, 0-12 to 0-7 on 50 minutes, the Kingdom were eyeing up that final spot. To Cork's credit they were battling away. Unlike their previous semi final clashes with their neighbour from across the county bounds Cork were not in the mood for capitulating.

Kerry though had more firepower in attack and on a few occasions carved open the Cork defence but were content to take their points. Donaghy's hard work was rewarded with a lovely point to stretch their lead to six and drew the biggest cheer of the day. The converted basketball player was now the new cult figure in the famed 'green and gold'.

Cork got the next two points from Sean O'Brien and Masters but they also undermined their hard work by failing to convert several opportunities. This included two '45's' which were expertly fielded by Dara O'Sé on the edge of his own square.

Colm Cooper then sealed a deserved win with two points and for the seventh time in ten years Kerry would be centre stage on All Ireland football final day, victors by 0-16 to 0-10. Cork manager Billy Morgan was highly critical of referee John Bannon afterwards but in truth he could have few complaints as his side were outfought by a Kerry team on a mission.

Semi Final

| Kerry | . . . . **0-16** |
| Cork | . . . . **0-10** |

Mayo v Dublin

It was never meant to be like this. Mayo were destined to fail again and Dublin were to progress to the dream final with old rivals Kerry. However, Mickey Moran's men never read the script and were singing from a different hymn sheet from the minute they set foot on the pitch.

This time the Dublin supporters were there early and watched as the drama began even before a ball was kicked in anger.

Having arrived on the field first and posed for the customary team photograph, Mayo then proceeded to commence their pre-match warm-up at the Hill 16 end of the ground – much to the amazement of the massed 'Dubs' congregated on the Hill, and also to their own team manager Mickey Moran. It was a players' decision and they were 'not for turning' as the saying goes.

Consternation then when Dublin emerged from the dressing room. They too headed for the Hill 16 end of the ground. The sight of over sixty players indulging in a pre-match routine in the same confined space only added spice to the riveting atmosphere within the stadium.

In the confusion that followed, Mayo's dietician, Mary McNicholas was knocked unconscious, accidentally, by a flying football. Mentors from both sides got involved in a little bit of shenanigans before it all settled

Ronan McGarrity, Mayo, fields the high ball
denying Ciaran Whelan, Dublin. Dublin v Mayo,
All Ireland Football Semi Final, Croke Park,
Dublin. 27 August 2006

down and the action got underway.

What followed for the next seventy minutes made the pre-match preamble look like a teddy bear's picnic as the drama of a classic contest unfolded before a spellbound capacity crowd of 82,500.

Dublin must have been affected by the histrionics prior to the start as they were left in the starting blocks as Mayo opened up a four point lead.

It later emerged that the Dublin team and management were informed by officials that Mayo had occupied the Hill 16 end of the ground. As they pondered their position, they actually delayed their entry to the field by four minutes. Manager Paul Caffrey and his selectors decided to go there (Hill 16) also. It was to prove a wrong call. Dublin and Caffrey were clearly rattled, as evidenced by the fact that Dublin failed to score for the opening 1 minutes.

Mayo's Ronan McGarrity and Pat Harte dominated midfield and with the Dublin defence under pressure, it was 0-5 to 0-1 after twenty minutes.

However, Dublin were right

back in the game on 23 minutes when Conal Keaney booted home a goal. It lifted their sagging spirits.

With momentum behind them, Dublin drove on. Keaney kicked a point when he could have taken a goal. Jason Sherlock hit the crossbar and Mayo defender Aidan Higgins denied Alan Brogan a goal with a great block. It was Mayo who were now in difficulty, but they steadied the ship and kicked two late points to lead at the interval by 0-9 to 1-5. By this stage Mayo had lost influential midfielder McGarrity who never really recovered from a tackle by Ciaran Whelan and the big Dublin midfielder was lucky to remain on the field. Time for players and supporters to draw breath as the sides trooped to the dressing room with rapturous applause ringing in their ears.

Dublin reshaped their team for the second half, and in a strange move they deployed Shane Ryan at right half-back. It was a switch that did not work. Ryan, who was excellent in midfield, never adjusted to his new role and was partly at fault for the Mayo goal. His lack of experience in a defensive role saw him exposed,

and eventually he was replaced. Only Paul Caffrey and his selectors can explain the rationale behind the move.

Initially the switch looked like working as Dublin took complete control on the resumption and in a blistering opening 11 minutes outscored Mayo by 1-6 to 0-1. Alan Brogan fired over three sublime points and had a hand in Dublin's second goal.

It was copybook stuff – the ball being transferred through several players at speed before Sherlock flicked it to the net. Kevin Bonner and Keaney added points and at 2-11 to 0-10, Mayo were in trouble. Dublin and their fanatical supporters were booking tickets for the final.

However this pulsating encounter had a bit to run yet, and unlike previous Mayo teams, this one was different. 'Faith' is what Moran described it as afterwards. In quick succession, the Derry-born Mayo boss introduced three substitutes – Andy Moran, David Brady and Aidan Kilcoyne along with another replacement Kevin O'Neill. It provided the right formula to unlock the Dubs. The fightback of the championship was underway, so much so that in a captivating closing quarter Dublin only managed one more score.

Mayo were galvanised by the changes and when Alan Dillon landed a couple of points they were back in the game. Then came the goal that set the scene for as dramatic a conclusion to a game as anyone would have wished for. Andy Moran was the scorer, his first in the Championship, on 51 minutes. Minutes later, points from Dillon and Conor Mortimer completed the turnaround. Mayo were in front 1-15 to 2-11 on 54 minutes.

For the next 11 minutes neither side managed a score as tired limbs battled might and main for the right to face Kerry. Alan Brogan's seventh point in the 66th minute had a replay looking a distinct possibility. But there was a few more twists left in this enthralling game yet.

Ciarán McDonald, the great enigma of Mayo football, proved the hero, as his shot from a difficult angle split the posts at the Hill 16 end. The Connacht champions were back in front.

Dublin came in search of the leveller. Sherlock won a '45', but by now regular free-taker Moss Quinn had been replaced and th

A Mayo football is left behind after both teams attempted to warm up on the same half of the pitch in front of Hill 16. Dublin v Mayo, All Ireland Football Semi Final, Croke Park, Dublin. 27 August 2006

task of squaring the match fell to Mark Vaughan. His effort was well directed but Mayo goalkeeper David Clarke got a hand to it and steered it away from the goal. It fell to Sherlock but his effort was blocked and the siege temporary lifted.

It looked safe for Mayo but they had to survive a few more minutes and once again Vaughan had a free to save his side. This time his effort sailed wide.

Seconds later the best game of football witnessed in years was brought to a conclusion by excellent referee Paddy Russell and Dublin's 11-year wait for a place in the final would go on.

Mayo, who last won the Sam Maguire Cup in 1951, were back in a final to face Kerry just as they did in 2004. Having evicted Dublin from Hill 16 at the start of the game, they had now completed the job and evicted them from the Championship race altogether.

Afterwards Mickey Moran said, 'it was the first time in my life that I felt my heart beat at a match'. His team showed they too had heart – in abundance.

Semi Final
Mayo **1-16**
Dublin **2-12**

Eddie Brennan, Kilkenny, catches a high ball while his team-mate James Fitzpatrick affords some protection from the advancing Sean Óg Ó hAilpín, Cork.
Cork v Kilkenny,
All Ireland Hurling Final,
Croke Park, Dublin.
3 September 2006

THE HURLING FINAL

Cork were going for three-in-a-row. Kilkenny who were denied three-in-a-row by Cork two years ago in 2004, were determined to stop them. 'It wasn't a factor,' said both managers. But were they right?

Cork v Kilkenny

It was an All Ireland Hurling Final with more than just the Liam McCarthy Cup on offer. Cork were going for three-in-a-row. Kilkenny were determined to deny them. In advance, both camps were keen to play down its significance. John Allen and Brian Cody said 'it wasn't a factor'.

It was there though, hovering like a dark cloud on a winter's day.

The search for tickets reached epic

proportions, yet on the day, as usual, they surfaced and most were catered for.

Kilkenny were dealt a huge blow earlier in the week when injury ruled excellent defender JJ Delaney out, while Donnacha Cody, son of manager Brian, also lost out with a knee injury.

The announcement of the teams set the scene. The weather conditions were favourable. Regrettably, the much criticised pitch once again looked below par for such a huge occasion.

Despite extensive work in the lead-up to the final, the grass, acknowledged by both sides afterwards, was much too high for hurling – the only blight on another exciting afternoon.

Inside the ground, Tipperary won the minor final with ease over Galway, and now the countdown was well underway. The Offaly team of 1981, who won the county's first hurling title, were introduced to the capacity crowd of 82,275. It evoked special memories as the names were reeled off. Coughlan, Kelly, Keeshan, Kirwan and a huge cheer for Brian Carroll, son of the late and lamented Pat, a hurler supreme.

Young boys and girls placed the cup on a podium as the 'Cats' and the 'Rebels' emerged from the dressing rooms, and it seemed as if all of Cork was in the ground. The stadium was awash with 'red and white' but only fifteen could play. The Kilkenny support was not found wanting as a gripping contest evolved over the next seventy minutes.

As the teams were introduced to President Mary McAleese, it was Kilkenny who looked the more relaxed. For once Kilkenny were underdogs. The pressure was all on Cork. That dark cloud (three-in-a-row) was still lingering in the air.

Formalities complete just after 3.30pm, referee Barry Kelly from Westmeath got the game underway. Kilkenny switched players in attack and defence, while Cork only made one positional change. The tactical manoeuvres were underway.

Henry Shefflin and Joe Deane traded points, but it was noticeable that there was an intensity about Kilkenny's play that Cork had not encountered all year. 'Hunger' was a word that immediately came to mind.

Manager Cody also had his

game plan – to stop Cork's running and passing style. Midfielder Derek Lyng was deployed as an extra defender, thereby denying Cork the space they craved.

There were times when Kilkenny resembled Armagh or Tyrone footballers as they engulfed the Cork player in possession with menacing intent. So with space at a premium, Cork could never develop their favoured support game that had undone so many teams in the past.

Shefflin and Aidan Fogarty edged Kilkenny two points ahead, an early statement of intent. Cork hit back. Niall McCarthy and John Tennyson squared up to one another, and then McCarthy landed a great point. Ben O'Connor and Deane had similar scores and Cork were in front 0-4 to 0-3.

Shefflin and Martin Comerford shared three points and Cork's lead was short-lived. In fact the champions were to go 14 minutes without a score. Deane pointed a free, quickly followed by a beauty from Ben O'Connor – level again. It may have lacked the quality expected from two hurling purists, but it was passionate, exciting and

intense with no quarter asked or given. Kilkenny were playing with a steely resolve, hunting, harassing and chasing every ball with a ravenous hunger. Cork were struggling to gain a foothold in the match. Their key men were having little impact on proceedings. It was like a chess game, and Cody was in control.

Shefflin and Deane swapped points, then a defining moment arrived.

Twenty-nine minutes played when the ball broke in the square. It fell into the grateful arms of Aidan Fogarty. Seconds later the umpire was reaching for the green flag as the sliotar nestled in the net. Goal for Kilkenny, who enjoyed an interval lead of 1-8 to 0-8. However it was the manner in which they were playing that would have given Brian Cody immense satisfaction.

Cork needed a good start to the second-half and John Allen made a couple of changes in an effort to lift their challenge. Their play though lacked the zip of previous matches and only a few players were playing up to the required standard. Kilkenny by contrast had star performers all over the field.

James Ryall, Noel Hickey and Tommy Walsh were magnificent in defence.

James 'Cha' Fitzpatrick was the dominant figure in midfield, while in attack it was fast developing into the Henry and Aidan show.

Shefflin had fitted neatly into the role normally occupied by the departed DJ Carey, leading the attack with purpose. Fogarty blossomed after scoring the goal and ended with a total of 1-3, and also picked up the 'man of the match' award.

Brian Murphy, Cork, tries to brush off the challenge of Richie Power, Kilkenny. Cork v Kilkenny, All Ireland Senior Hurling Final, Croke Park, Dublin. 3 September 2006

Unheralded before the game, hero afterwards.

Cork were struggling. Little cameos around the field were going against them. Passes that would normally be inch perfect were falling short, while one or two others drifted over the sideline. There was a sense that it was not going to be their day. Yet with only eleven minutes remaining they were still within touching distance, trailing by just three points 1-12 to 0-12.

Kilkenny had shot some poor wides but in the space of three minutes, they doubled their advantage.

Eddie Brennan and Fogarty had points from play and when the imperious Shefflin landed his seventh point from a free the gap was now six, 1-15 to 0-12. Shefflin's clinched fist to the Kilkenny supporters on Hill 16 was an indication that the title was theirs.

Ben O'Connor, Cork's best forward, landed a free, Shefflin replied, but the champions' hopes were fading fast. Then from nowhere they were given a glimmer of hope.

Four minutes from time Niall McCarthy worked hard to create a chance for Ben O'Connor who drilled an unstoppable shot to the net. The stadium exploded. Cork were back in the game. Could they pull something out of the bag, as the stewards took up end-of-match positions?

Seconds later Shefflin missed a reasonably easy free. On the sideline Cody looked on in disbelief, he knew it was the game breaker.

Cork, with two minutes of added time to be played, had one last chance but the Kilkenny defence were not going to be caught again. Seconds later it was all over with Kilkenny champions by a single score 1-16 to 1-13, but in truth it could and should have been more.

Jubilation for the men from the Marble County, despair for the fallen champions whose cherished three-in-a-row ambitions lay in tatters. A role reversal of their last meeting in 2004, when Cork denied Kilkenny their first ever three-in-a-row. That was a defeat that hurt Kilkenny and avenging it provided them with extra motivation. History, they say, is hard to make.

Despite the best efforts of stewards and gardaí alike, the crowds made their way onto the pitch to engulf their heroes. John Allen, ever the sportsman, seeks out and shakes Brian Cody's hand. The Kilkenny manager, cut from the same cloth as Allen, acknowledges and appreciates the gesture.

Eventually fighting his way through the masses, Jackie Tyrell climbs the most famous steps in Irish sport, to be greeted by a beaming President. It's a proud moment for Nickey Brennan, a short few months in office. He hands the Liam McCarthy Cup to a fellow Kilkenny man. The enduring image of Nickey cradling the cup in his arms as Jackie makes his speech, says it all.

Kilkenny are champions for the 29th time. The huge crowd underneath the Hogan Stand acknowledge the new champions, a far cry from three years ago, when they accepted the cup in an almost deserted stadium. The mini famine in a hurling mad county was over.

In the media scrum that engulfed him afterwards, Brian Cody hit back at his critics. 'The disappointing thing is that a lot was said during the year that wasn't exactly genuine, some of

Kilkenny supporters break through to run on to the pitch as the full-time whistle blows. Cork v Kilkenny, All Ireland Hurling Final, Croke Park, Dublin. 3 September 2006

our players were not up to it; Noel Hickey was too slow for Croke Park; the people that were writing us off can now change their tune.'

Cody hailed the defensive effort as a primary factor in winning the title, his fourth in eight years as manager. 'The best skill in hurling is to tackle, block and put pressure on players. We did that today and maintained it for the entire match.'

He also made reference to the team's hunger. 'The hunger to win an All Ireland is something. It's the 'be all and end all' for every player. That and our spirit is the cornerstone of our set-up and spirit drives us on.' With that he was off with a spring in his step.

Meanwhile, gracious as ever Cork's John Allen offers no excuses. 'We were beaten by the better team on the day and have no complaints really. We did not play well; were not allowed play and we congratulate Kilkenny on their win, but I am proud of our team and they have the character to bounce back from this defeat.'

The inevitable question about his own future followed. 'That's for another day, it's a huge commitment now to manage an inter-county team. I will discuss it

Kilkenny captain Jackie Tyrell lifts the Liam McCarthy Cup. Cork v Kilkenny, All Ireland Hurling Final, Croke Park, Dublin. 3 September 2006

with my family and colleagues and make a decision in a couple of weeks.'

Long after the crowds had left, Brian Cody walked across the almost deserted Croke Park pitch with the Liam McCarthy Cup in his hand. A handful of Kilkenny supporters waved. He held the cup aloft and shouted 'brilliant'.

It is indeed. As the inter-county hurling season inhales its last breath, Kilkenny end it unbeaten, as they march to glory in all four competitions they competed in. Walsh Cup, National League, Leinster Championship and finally the biggest prize of all – the Guinness All Ireland Senior Championship. All trophies now reside down by 'Mooncoin'.

Hurling Final
Kilkenny **1-16**
Cork **1-13**

A player places a sliotar for a free.

A Special Day In
CROKE PARK
THE CAMOGIE and UNDER 21 FINALS

September 10, 2006, was an historic day in Croke Park. For the first time the Camogie and Under 21 finals are both the featured events.

Sunday September 10th, 2006 was an historic occasion in Croke Park. It was a day in which the GAA and the Camogie Association came together as one, in a manner of speaking. It may have happened before with a major hurling game and a camogie final on the same programme, but this time it was pre-planned and scheduled.

For years the All Ireland Senior Camogie

inal and the Under 21 Hurling inal clashed. Very often counties vere doubly engaged and families livided, but this year no such oroblems existed.

It is all part of the integration oolicy being pursued by the three nain bodies within the GAA. In he coming years, all will work losely together for the betterment of all three.

Sean Kelly made it a plank of is presidency, clearly recognising he growing influence both amogie and ladies' football were aving on units of the GAA.

The Camogie Association is ow in its 102nd year and have ut in place new structures that ill guide it toward its second entury. These new and well-nought out ideas will not be seen o good effect in the immediate uture but the long-term objectives re certain to be attained.

In many respects the Senior amogie Championship mirrors nat of the Hurling hampionships with only a small umber of genuine contenders.

Time was when Dublin was the ominant county. Now they ply neir trade in Junior, likewise ntrim who have a rich tradition the game. Kilkenny, with the

Downey twins Ann and Angela, won 12 titles in 13 years, but have not tasted success since 1994.

Galway raised their head above the parapet briefly to claim the title in 1996 – scant reward for all the good work at under-age level.

That leaves us with Cork and Tipperary who between them have shared the last eight championships, the latter with five, having won their first in 1999. Cork are the reigning champions and make no secret of their desire to add to the 21 titles they have won to date.

Over the years various formats were devised in an effort to make it a more competitive championship and once again as the 2006 campaign got underway, it had a new format and a new sponsor.

Gala, the supermarket chain, took over and to their credit were a very active and visible sponsor. It was launched amid a blaze of publicity, as the race to be part of an historic occasion got underway.

This year all six top flight counties were grouped together, with the top four qualifying for the semi finals. It was hoped this would give the championship a fresh impetus.

Champions Cork guaranteed their place in the last four with three wins on the trot. Tipperary and Galway had also secured their places as the final series of games got underway, leaving Leinster rivals Kilkenny and Wexford in a battle for the last spot.

Both sides won their respective games, but Kilkenny grabbed the semi final berth with a victory over Galway.

The semi final draw decreed that Cork would play Galway with Kilkenny meeting Tipperary. Nowlan Park, Kilkenny was the venue for both games on Saturday August 12th.

Champions Cork were always in control, even if it took them 19 minutes to open their account, but they were playing against a strong wind. Emer Dillon scored a crucial goal in the 23rd minute and they led 1-3 to 0-3 at half-time. Lourda Kavanagh was Galway's lone scorer.

Cork retained the initiative on the resumption and with four unanswered points eased into a winning position. Galway did mount a late rally that yielded three points, but it was not enough and Cork triumphed by 1-7 to 0-6.

The second semi final was a much more fluid affair and despite Kilkenny putting in a huge effort, Tipperary always looked likely winners. Although they were grateful to goalkeeper Jovita Delaney who made two excellent saves in the second half when Kilkenny were on top.

Tipperary led by 0-7 to 0-5 at half-time, but an up-and-coming Kilkenny side made them work hard in the second half and were boosted by a goal from Maire Dargan. However, Delaney denied them further glory with crucial saves as Tipperary held on to win by 0-13 to 1-8.

A new sponsor, a new format but a familiar pairing on final day - Cork v Tipperary. Fitting perhaps that the modern-day specialists should usher in a new era for camogie.

Erin Under 21 Hurling

It was first played for in 1964 and in that period has produced some classic encounters at both provincial and national level. Despite helping to bridge the gap between minor and senior, there have been repeated calls over the years for this grade to be abandoned. Various reasons are put forward, the most common one is its interference with several other grades. So far those responsible have resisted the temptation to succumb to such pressure and it is hoped that they never will. It may not be ideal but it's a Championship that has served all counties well and no doubt will continue to do so in the coming years.

Surprising then that it was only last year that the Championship found a sponsor, with Erin Foods giving the competition a further boost with their support.

As with the Senior Championship, Leinster and Munster provide the major participants. Ulster is confined to Down and Antrim, the latter winning this year's title. Galway are the sole standard bearers from Connacht and enter at the semi final stage. They make light of this difficulty and have a good record at this level and were champions in 2005.

Tipperary triumph in Munster
No real surprise that Cork and Tipperary contested the Munster final. The great rivals met in all four provincial deciders this year. The pressure was on Tipperary to stop Cork's bid for a second successive clean sweep of Munster hurling titles.

On the night and before a crowd of over 5,000 in Semple Stadium, Thurles, Tipperary's ability to poach goals at crucial times ended Cork's ambitions.

Darragh Egan, Darragh Hickey and Ray McLoughney were the goal scorers that helped breathe life back into Tipperary hurling and end their wait for a Munster title. Antrim now stood between them and a place in the All Ireland Final.

Kilkenny again in Leinster
The only real drama in Leinster came in the final, where Dublin, making strides in underage hurling, tested the raging hot favourites, and were aggrieved at a decision that unhinged their efforts. Kilkenny looked in control at half-time as they led by 1-10 to 0-4. Dublin had been reduced to 14 men in the 28th minute when midfielder Willie Lowry was dismissed by Meath referee Fergus Smith. Smith flashed a second yellow card at Lowry. This incensed Dublin officials who were adamant that he had not been yellow carded earlier. They were correct.

Undaunted, Dublin battled back and reduced the deficit to three points, but a 56th minute goal by David McCormack ended their brave resistance.

It came as little consolation to the crestfallen Dublin players that when submitting his report to the Leinster Council, the referee admitted he erred in sending off Lowry. Dublin sought a replay. Kilkenny had little objection but the Council refused and a hard-done Dublin were left to rue a major blunder that may have cost them a badly-needed title. Kilkenny meanwhile move on to an All Ireland Semi Final with reigning champions Galway the team that beat them in the 2005 final.

Comfortable wins in Semi Finals
There was little excitement in the semi finals. Tipperary were always in control of their clash with Antrim. It was 1-12 to 0-2 at half-time and the Munster champions used their full complement of substitutes as they ran out convincing winners by 5-19 to 0-7.

Much was expected of the clash between Kilkenny and champions Galway in the splendidly renovated O'Connor Park, Tullamore.

Galway had 18-year-old Joe Canning on the bench, who on September 3rd would be bidding for his third All Ireland minor medal in a row. The arrangement was to bring him on only if needed.

Twenty-one minutes gone, he was needed. Kilkenny were 1-8 to 0-4 ahead, Richie Power getting the goal. Canning's first touch produced a goal and he quickly added a point, but Kilkenny were still in control 1-12 to 1-5 at half-time.

Canning was to score a second goal, but Kilkenny with some sublime points from James 'Cha' Fitzpatrick, TJ Reid and Philly Hogan eased to a comfortable win by 1-24 to 2-12, and now their keenest rivals Tipperary awaited in the final.

Drama in Hurling Final
In their programme notes both GAA President Nickey Brennan and Camogie President Liz Howard endorsed the 'integration' of the Under 21 and Camogie Final on a two-year trial period and were looking forward to witnessing two cracking games.

The young hurlers of Kilkenny and Tipperary were first into action before a crowd of 20,685, on a pitch that was in much better condition than it was for the Senior Hurling Final a week earlier.

It helped produce a classic contest between two counties whose rivalry is as intense as any in the GAA.

Kilkenny had three senior stars in their side, while Tipperary were bidding to add this title to the minor championship won the previous week.

Within thirty seconds, TJ Reid had a Kilkenny point and with 'Cha' Fitzpatrick hitting some lovely frees, the Leinster champions made the better start. Tipperary though were undaunted and with James Woodlock and Stephen Lillis doing well in midfield they battled back. Darragh Egan matched Fitzpatrick with his free-taking and only one point separated the sides at half-time, Kilkenny with the slender advantage 0-9 to 0-8.

The second half turned into an absorbing battle as the play swung from end to end. The lead changed hands several times and it also produced four quality goals.

Egan got the first for Tipperary with a blistering free in the 36th minute. It helped Tipperary to a 1-13 to 0-13 lead.

There was only five more scores added in the remaining time, but that did not lessen the quality of the game as it ebbed and flowed. Then the goals arrived.

Kilkenny crafted their first in the 48th minute. Richie Power was on the end of a sweet move and his blistering drive billowed the back of the net. Three minutes later substitute Richie Hogan landed a peach of a point from under the Hogan Stand – Kilkenny back in front.

Egan levelled it with a point before Niall Teehan's persistence was rewarded with a Tipperary goal seven minutes from time, 2-14 to 1-14, and the Munster champions in sight of their ninth title and first since 1995.

Kilkenny laid siege to the Tipperary goal but were thwarted by the brilliance of goalkeeper Gerry Kennedy, who made three fabulous saves and looked to have steered his side to victory.

The clock was inching its way to the third and final minute of injury time when the 'Cats' launched one last attack. The ball landed in the square amid a cluster of hurleys and young Richie Hogan was quickest to react. This time Kennedy could only watch as the ball rattled the back of the net. Goal, level again and little time for anything else, except the puck out. It was the last act of a dramatic encounter. Tipperary players were devastated at having victory snatched from their grasp. Kilkenny were elated at salvaging a draw when it looked as if the die was cast.

Referee Michael Haverty called time, sending both sides to Thurles a week later for an eagerly awaited replay.

A terrific start to an historic afternoon, and in a frenetic finish very few realised that Kilkenny ended the game with fourteen men after substitute Maurice Nolan was sent off, with a straight red card.

Another thrilling encounter

A week after the thriller in Croke Park, Semple Stadium was the venue for another instalment in the Kilkenny v Tipperary rivalry.

To accommodate the crowd of 18,578 the start was delayed for ten minutes. But it was worth the wait as both sides delivered another quality contest.

It was a contest full of commitment which lasted the entire 60 minutes, and once again almost produced a dramatic finish.

Kilkenny led by 0-4 to 0-2 after fifteen minutes with senior star Richie Power among the scorers. With Darragh Egan showing up well for Tipperary, the home side had edged ahead. Then came the decisive score.

In a tight game goals were always going to be crucial and so it proved. Austin Murphy provided the pass and Paddy Hogan's finish was clinical. That goal put Kilkenny back in front at half-time 1-6 to 0-7. It was a lead they would not relinquish.

The second half never relented in intensity. Scores were scarce as the defending on both sides was of the highest standard.

Tipperary made valiant efforts to pull the game out of the fire and had one last opportunity when they were awarded a close-in free in injury time.

Egan discarded the helmet as he was faced by a wall of Kilkenny defenders, but his powerful shot was diverted to safety before the full-time whistle sounded. Kilkenny 1-11 Tipperary 0-11.

Mary O'Connor, Cork, tries to break through the attempted blocking by Geraldine Kinane, Emily Hayden, left, and Louise Young, Tipperary. Cork v Tipperary, All Ireland Senior Camogie Final, Croke Park. 10 September 2006.

The famed Cashel Cross Trophy was heading out of its spiritual home on the short journey to the Marble County. A second All Ireland title for the 'Cats' in the space of six days.

Enter the Ladies

Following such a dramatic finish, the camogie players of Cork and Tipperary had a hard act to follow, as the pre-match routine got underway.

The occasion was graced by the presence of the President Mary McAleese, herself a former camogie player, and as ever she was warmly received by the crowd. The Camogie Final day is different, and this was still the main feature, in that it is well attended by groups of young and enthusiastic spectators, who generate their own special atmosphere. Whistles, horns, bugles and other little objects make various degrees of noise as the teams are introduced and then indulge in the pre-match parade. The noise continued for the duration of the game.

Tipperary supporters although clearly in the majority, were strangely subdued, still stunned by the dramatic end to the hurling final shortly before.

Cork looked fresh and lively and imposed themselves on proceedings from the start. It was evident from very early on that the Cork defence were in outstanding form, and as the game progressed so did their control.

The first point arrived in the ninth minute from Emer Dillon, the second from Jennifer O'Leary and Cork were in front. Indeed only the excellence of Tipperary goalkeeper Jovita Delaney denied Cork a goal when she deflected O'Leary's effort over the bar.

Tipperary, who were struggling, were given hope when Emily Hayden landed their opening point. Cork had set their stall out from the outset. It began in their half-back line with Rena Buckley,

Mary O'Connor (appearing in her ninth final) and Anna Geary building a reputation usually reserved for their male counterparts. It was the cornerstone of a defensive performance that was to frustrate Tipperary for the afternoon, and provided Cork with the platform for victory.

Behind this trio, captain Joanne O'Callaghan kept a tight rein on the dangerous Emer McDonnell, while Catriona Foley and Amanda O'Regan were equally efficient.

Briege Corkery and O'Leary had Cork points, before the hard working Joanne Ryan had Tipperary's first score in 11 minutes. Cork's control was strengthened further when O'Leary had her third point, quickly followed by a quality strike from Gemma O'Connor, now dominating with Corkery in midfield.

McDonnell, for the one and only time, slipped her marker to land a lovely point. It left the challengers trailing by 0-6 to 0-3 at half-time, and a mountain to climb in the second half.

Recognising their problems, Tipperary reshaped their team on the resumption. By the end, three of the starting six forwards had been withdrawn.

Cork, stung by the suggestion that they were fortunate to have just caught up with Tipperary in last year's final, were in no mood to let up and quickly set about re-asserting their control. Rachel Moloney, Una O'Donoghue and O'Leary tacked on points without reply and Tipperary were now staring a heavy defeat in the face.

As the closing quarter approached, Tipperary went in search of goals in an effort to breathe life back into their fast fading challenge, but all to no avail. The Cork defence adopted a 'thou shall not pass' mode. On the few occasions that they were passed, they found Aoife Murray unbeatable and the Cork goalkeeper pulled off three quality saves.

Ten minutes from time Cork had extended their lead with points from O'Donoghue and O'Connor. In the Hogan Stand, the 'red and white' ribbons were being put on the O'Duffy Cup and the only issue to be decided was the winning margin.

Cork's final score, and their only one from a free, came courtesy of O'Leary in the 59th minute, and it

was now 0-12 to 0-3. Tipperary had yet to score in the second half, with the game heading for the first goalless final in seventy-five years. Their total (0-4) was the lowest since Antrim failed to score in 1944.

Eventually they did register a score from Hayden in the third minute of injury time, but that did little for a Tipperary side that were comprehensively outplayed by a Cork side, with a point to prove.

Referee Fintan McNamara did an excellent job with his decision to let the game flow. The game ended with Cork winners by 0-12 to 0-4 and it was a proud Joanne O'Callaghan who would collect the most prized cup in camogie.

So yet another camogie championship concludes, with in all probability the ending of one dynasty (Tipperary were appearing in their eighth consecutive final), and the beginning of a new one. Such was the comprehensive nature of Cork's win and with a young and vibrant squad available, they look set to be the game's new standard bearers.

Triumph also for the backroom team, in particular John Cronin and former star Fiona O'Driscoll, who have now won back-to-back titles.

Afterwards O'Driscoll paid tribute to all the players for their efforts during the year. 'They have been superb and deserve whatever accolades come their way. We arrived here today determined to retain our title and we are delighted to have attained our goal.'

Tipperary boss Paddy McCormack offered no excuses, 'no complaints well beaten by the better team on the day'.

Cork now stand on the cusp of history, with the three-in-a-row in sight, but O'Driscoll was dismissing such thoughts.

'We will enjoy tonight and the next few days, let 2007 take care of itself.'

Shades of the Cork hurlers who were in a similar position as 2006 dawned but Fiona and her colleagues will hope to go one step further. However, that is for another day, as Cork bask in the glory of being crowned All Ireland Senior Champions for the 22nd time.

It brings the curtain down on a special day in HQ. It can be deemed a success and looks set to become a permanent arrangement.

The Kerry and Mayo teams parade around the pitch before the start of the game. Kerry v Mayo, All Ireland Senior Football Final, Croke Park, Dublin. 17 September 2006

THE KINGDOM MEETS MAYO

Kerry seek their 34th title while Mayo, buoyant after their thrilling semi final victory over Dublin, are hoping to end a 55-year famine.

The setting was perfect. A Sunday in September bathed in sunshine as 82,289 waited in anticipation of a classic final. Kerry were bidding for a 34th title while Mayo were hoping the famine that has lasted since 1951 would finally come to an end.

Mayo's great win over Dublin had raised expectations that this was a different team, one that would not lie down easily, while Kerry had quietly gone about their business since losing the Munster Final replay to Cork.

Press nights for both sides are well attended by key players who speak freely about their hopes for the final. Meanwhile the search for the elusive tickets was relentless. Two big 'immigrant' counties who command massive support, for many it would be a fruitless search.

The respective team announcements evoked more debate – 35-year-old Kevin O'Neill wins a recall for Mayo while in Kerry just a slight hint of controversy.

Declan O'Sullivan is named on the '40' to the exclusion of Eoin Brosnan and as a consequence, assumes the captaincy as is his right. The 'Gooch' would not, after all, captain Kerry in an All Ireland Final, yet. It's a gamble by Kerry manager Jack O'Connor as they are both Dromid-Pearses' clubmen in South Kerry – the reigning county champions.

More drama on the Wednesday before the

game. Reports emerge from Mayo that star forward Ciarán McDonald is doubtful with an injury. Immediately manager Mickey Moran issues a denial, but the rumours persist. By Thursday the rumour mill has gone into overdrive. Even some members of the Mayo panel privately admit that there is a problem. However, as expected, McDonald plays, but it's a nice little filler for the hacks as stories begin to run dry in the build-up to the final.

Sunday arrives and the scene is set with a cracking minor match.

Aidan O'Mahony, Kerry, successfully curbs the contribution of talisman Ciarán McDonald, Mayo. Kerry v Mayo, All Ireland Senior Football Final, Croke Park. 17 September 2006

It ended level between Kerry and Roscommon. The cup is put in storage for another week.

Brothers who won All Ireland medals on the same day in the last ten years are introduced to the crowd. Some famous names step forward. Downeys from Derry, Joyces from Galway, McHughs from Donegal and of course the O'Sé's from Kerry, who are represented by family members as Tomás, Marc and Dara have more pressing matters to occupy their minds for now.

A nice touch too before the game as Nickey Brennan and Liam Mulvihill on behalf of the GAA make a presentation to Ronnie Delaney to honour his gold medal achievement of fifty years ago at the Melbourne Olympics in 1956. Delaney receives a wonderful welcome from the crowd as the race appears on the big screen. The hour of reckoning for Kerry and Mayo is nearly at hand.

To a crescendo of noise the teams appear on the field. Kerry supporters are relaxed and confident while Mayo fans are nervous and hopeful.

President Mary McAleese meets the teams as the band plays the *Star of the County Down*. They parade and play *Amhrán Na bhFiann* to follow. The clock at the Canal End of the ground is inching ever nearer to 3.30pm. The waiting is almost over – no place to hide now!

It's also a special day for the referee, army officer Brian Crowe from Cavan who is about to get the biggest football match of the year underway.

Mayo get possession in the opening play of the game but it takes several passes as they try to clear the ball from defence. Kerry intercept it and in a flash Mike Frank Russell splits the posts with a point. First blood to the Kingdom. It sets the trend for the remainder of the afternoon.

In the third minute Mayo win a close-in free. Given that there is a point on offer, they take it quickly but an effort at a goal is well stopped by goalkeeper Diarmuid Murphy. A bad move – it would be another twelve minutes before the Connacht champions open their account.

In the interim, the new sensation of Kerry football, Kieran Donaghy, leaves his mark on this final. Seven minutes played he takes and gives a pass to team captain Declan O'Sullivan, who drills an unstoppable shot to the net. Kerry supporters had barely settled back into their seats when they were on their feet again.

This time Donaghy makes a spectacular catch, shrugs off the challenge of David Heaney and once again the rigging is almost ripped from the post such was the power of Donaghy's shot.

Kerry 2-4 Mayo 0-0. There and then the game died on its feet.

Stunned Mayo boss Mickey Moran withdraws centre-back James Nallen, O'Sullivan's direct opponent. O'Connor's gamble had paid dividends. David Brady was deployed to try and curb Donaghy and to a degree he succeeded, but it was a case of closing the stable door after the horse had bolted.

Mayo finally opened their account when Kevin O'Neill got in for a 16th minute goal. Kerry though were awesome in their approach and played like a team seeking their very first title, epitomised by the play of the so-called 'veterans' in their team.

Dara O'Sé and Tommy Griffin outplayed Pat Harte and Ronan McGarrity in midfield. Seamus Moynihan was his imperious best at centre-back and his 'reading' of the game was exceptional. The Glenflesk man also took time to fist a point when he might have had a goal, at a period when Mayo were in freefall.

Aidan O'Mahony was given the task of curbing Mayo's talisman Ciarán McDonald. He performed his duty to perfection, and even outscored his direct opponent by two points to one.

It got worse for Mayo when Colm Cooper availed of some dreadful defending to knock in goal number three. Thirty minutes played and there was a surreal look to the scoreboard – Kerry 3-7 Mayo 1-1.

There was a strange feeling in the stadium, almost eerie in fact, some finding the events unfolding on the field hard to believe.

Briefly, Mayo raised the hopes of their supporters. McDonald pointed a free, and in quick succession Pat Harte and Kevin O'Neill struck for goals. It was now 3-7 to 3-2 a bit more respectable. Crucially Declan O'Sullivan closed the first half – scoring a point to give Kerry a six point lead at the interval.

Time to draw breath, digest the opening 35 minutes of an

extraordinary All Ireland final that already had an air of inevitability about it.

For the game to take on any semblance of a contest Mayo needed a good start to the second half, but the opposite happened.

McDonald, a pale shadow of himself, missed with three chances, misses that drained whatever resistance was left in the Connacht champions. The body language told its own tale, they were a spent force.

It was a long and dreary thirty-five minutes, especially for Mayo who only managed three points in that period, all from frees by Conor Mortimer. In fact they only scored one point from play all afternoon – an indication of the difficulties they were experiencing.

Kerry, meanwhile, content that the title was in the bag started to empty the bench, although one tactical switch was made at half-time when Eoin Brosnan replaced Tomás O'Sé. Brosnan, Cooper and Bryan Sheehan got among the point scorers.

However the biggest cheer of the day arrived when Donaghy landed a massive point with the sands of time running out. It was greeted with a thunderous roar from the vast Kerry support.

The contest was long done and dusted when Kerry's fourth goal arrived courtesy of Brosnan in injury time. By then the rows of empty seats dotted around the stadium told its own story as did the scoreline. Kerry 4-15 Mayo 3-5.

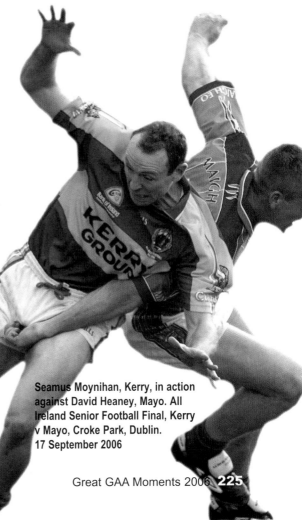

Seamus Moynihan, Kerry, in action against David Heaney, Mayo. All Ireland Senior Football Final, Kerry v Mayo, Croke Park, Dublin. 17 September 2006

Once again the stewards were unable to keep the fans off the field as 'green and gold' clad supporters raced on to greet their heroes – a far cry from the Munster championship when they were noticeable only by their absence. But this was special.

The team and management had responded to the criticism both from within and outside the county and delivered an emphatic answer to those who said there was disharmony in the camp.

Donaghy's presence on the edge of the square transformed their season and they are worthy All Ireland champions. A triumph too for manager Jack O'Connor, who now has won two titles in three years. Add in two league titles and two Munster championships – not bad for a guy who never won an All Ireland medal but has proved himself a quality coach at all levels – college, division, club and county.

It was a proud Declan O'Sullivan, joined on the rostrum by Colm Cooper, who accepted the Sam Maguire Cup from Nickey Brennan. It was the end of a journey that had many twists and turns along the way, but ultimately ended gloriously and in spectacular style.

Afterwards Jack O'Connor admitted it was special; 'we were written off a lot of times, some of the criticism was unfair but you answer your critics on the field and we did that today'.

O'Connor also said they had extra motivation, 'we desperately wanted to win for Seamus (Moynihan) and Dara (O'Sé), and give them their fourth medal, while 'Gooch' had only one coming into today. We had loads of reasons to motivate ourselves and we also wanted to make up for last year's defeat.'

As for Mayo, another hugely disappointing day on the day that really matters. It will take something special to lift this group of players again. Two heavy defeats at the hands of Kerry will have done little for confidence. What of their fans? The wait, the suffering and the famine is extended for another year at least.

But the day and the glory belong to the aristocrats of football. Kerry, another double of league and championship and 'Sam' heads back to An Ríocht to spend the autumn and winter visiting familiar friends and places.

The curtain comes down on

Kerry captain Declan O'Sullivan and stand-in captain Colm Cooper, right, lift the Sam Maguire Cup. Kerry v Mayo, All Ireland Senior Football Final, Croke Park, Dublin. 17 September 2006

another championship and possibly on the careers of some of the game's outstanding players. Seamus Moynihan actually retired within the week and Dara Ó'Sé is contemplating doing likewise. Jack O'Connor and his backroom team may also step down.

What a way to go – as champions, yet again!

Kay O'Reilly, Laois, gets her pass away while being tackled by Norita Kelly, Cork. Cork v Laois, Ladies All Ireland Football Semi Final, O'Connor Park, Tullamore, Co. Offaly. 2 September 2006.

LADIES' FOOTBALL
A GROWING SPORT

One of the fastest growing sports in the country, Ladies' Football is now enjoying a period of unprecedented growth.

It is now among one of the fastest growing sports in the country and it is easy to see why. Ladies' Football is enjoying a period of unprecedented growth. Clubs are springing up in all counties, and the counties themselves are responding. Even Kilkenny, not exactly renowned for their love of the 'big ball', compete in the National League, unlike their male counterparts. It may be in Division 4, but as the saying goes, 'from little acorns grow big trees'.

Early attempts to get the sport off the ground met with little success but in 1974 it began in earnest. While only a few counties participated in the initial competitions, that has changed dramatically with the passing of time.

All thirty-two counties compete in a four Division National League that has the backing of sponsors Suzuki. The All Ireland Championship is run along similar lines to the male competition, although without the qualifiers. The four provincial councils organise their own championships with the winners and runners-up then playing in the All Ireland quarter finals.

Both Senior and Junior Championships are sponsored by TG4, whose comprehensive coverage of the games has added a new dimension to a fledging competition.

As with all sports it has seen good and bad times. These days are definitely good.

However, it is not all about the Senior All Ireland championship. The Ladies' Football Association also runs competitions at all grades right down to under 12 at inter-county level. The various grades for clubs are also catered for with the All Ireland series in senior, junior and intermediate.

A quick glance at the records will show that over the years one county and one club have tended to dominate at different times, probably a reflection of the lack of serious opposition in that period. This is no longer the case. As the game spreads its wings, the honours' list continues to produce new names.

In the All Ireland Championship, Kerry, not surprisingly, was the first dynasty to emerge, winning the Brendan Martin Cup for a record nine years in a row between 1982 and 1991.

Waterford stepped in for two in 1992 and 1993, before the Kingdom Ladies won again in 1994. Kerry has not tasted success since.

Between 1994 and 1998, Waterford and Monaghan were the dominant teams, both winning two titles each, but neither managed a coveted three-in-a-row.

They were to meet in four finals out of five, and in many ways were responsible for a major change in the game, principally because of the 1997 decider.

It is a game that is now part of Ladies' Football folklore and is still talked about today. At the end of 60 minutes Waterford were ahead. Two minutes into injury time they were still in front and looked set for victory.

Incredibly, the referee proceeded to play another nine minutes, eleven in total, and Monaghan snatched the title in dramatic fashion to win by two points leaving Waterford stunned.

When the sides met again in the following year's final (1998), the clock and hooter had been introduced, thereby removing the time factor from the referee. This is now controlled by sideline officials who stop the clock at every stoppage in the game, guaranteeing the full sixty minutes is played. On reaching the allotted time, the hooter sounds and unless a free has been awarded the match is finished. It has proved to be a resounding success.

The enduring rivalry between these two counties propelled the game into the eyes of the public, who quickly sat up and took notice. Suddenly it was fashionable to play and follow Ladies' Football.

Mayo was the next county to inscribe their name on the roll of honour, winning four titles in five years. Laois broke Mayo's sequence of wins by capturing their one and only championship in 2001.

In the Senior Club Championship one name sticks out, Ballymacabry, a tiny little hamlet in county Waterford. What a team they were, as they carved out a special niche for themselves in their chosen sport.

What they achieved will surely never be equalled let alone surpassed. In a twelve year period they were crowned champions ten times, including a seven-in-a-row from 1989 to 1995. They lost out in 1996, but came back again in '97 and '98 to claim two further titles.

Off the field the sport continues to prosper. All-Star teams were first selected in 1981, and these continue to the present day. However, a ground-breaking decision two years ago has elevated these awards to a much higher status.

In 2004, the Ladies Football All-Stars travelled to New York and played a two-game series, while this was followed in 2006 with a trip to Singapore, where another exhibition game took place much to the delight of the Irish contingent in that sprawling city.

As the 2006 Championship got underway, Cork the reigning champions were installed as favourites to retain their title, reinforced when the Leeside ladies put league titles back-to-back by beating Meath in the final.

The big surprise in the provincial championship came in Ulster where last year's Junior All Ireland champions, Armagh, defeated the once powerful Monaghan in the final. It was the first time in the history of the championship that the Junior champions made such an impact in their inaugural year at senior. The Orchard county ladies would turn a few more heads before the season ran its course.

In Leinster, Meath, building on their good league campaign, made it to the final, but were unable to maintain that momentum and lost out to Laois.

Mayo and Galway have dominated the male football championship in the west and now the ladies are in a similar position as they contested the final. This time Galway atoned for the defeat of their male counterparts to record a win as the 2004 All Ireland champions gear themselves for another tilt at the title.

As expected Cork were too good for the challengers in Munster and eased to another title, beating former kingpins Waterford in a one-sided final.

Quarter Final drama

The stage was now set for the last eight of an exciting championship as the race for the Brendan Martin Cup gathered pace. 1974 was the first year that this cup was played for, donated by Brendan, one of the founding members of the association. The Offaly man has been a lifelong supporter of Ladies' Football and can regularly be seen attending games at venues throughout the country. The original cup was replaced with a bigger version in 1997, and once again Brendan was the benefactor.

Armagh's drive for glory continued in this round when they produced a fabulous display to end Waterford's ambitions. Sharon Duncan got a first half goal to help her side to an interval lead of 1-5 to 0-4. The pivotal moment of the game arrived early in the second half when Armagh goalkeeper Fionnuala McAntamney saved Linda Wall's penalty.

It gave Armagh the confidence they needed and they tacked on a few points before sealing a 2-10 to 0-9 win with a late goal from Maire O'Donnell. The Armagh dream was very much alive.

Cork were too good for Mayo winning by 2-12 to 1-11, the Connacht girls were not helped as they were reduced to fourteen players for the last ten minutes when Cora Staunton on receipt of a yellow card was sent to the sin bin.

Monaghan never really recovered from their defeat to Armagh in the Ulster final and were easily beaten 4-11 to 2-7 by Laois.

Without doubt, the best game in the quarter finals was the clash of Galway and Meath, which took extra-time and eventually a replay to decide. The first game saw Galway open up a commanding lead of nine points at one stage. However, they were pegged back by the resilient Royal ladies. Meath forced extra-time but the issue remained unresolved and it ended all square Galway 3-11

Meath 1-17.

The replay a week later was just as exciting. Meath buoyed by their comeback in the drawn game opened up a 0-7 to 0-3 lead with Gillian Bennett prominent in the scoring. Galway were sparked into life when Edel Concannon pounced for a 23rd minute goal to reduce the Meath lead.

Undaunted Meath surged ahead on the resumption, before Gillian Joyce (she finished with 1-6) lashed in Galway's second goal.

Meath made valiant efforts to draw level and cut the deficit to a point but when the hooter sounded, Galway had done enough to make the semi final, narrowly 2-10 to 0-15.

Controversy in Semi Finals

Contrasting games in the semi finals – drama and excitement in one, while the other is a mundane affair as Cork reach their second successive final.

There was never much doubt about the outcome as Laois could not match Cork's greater craft and experience. Outstanding corner-forward Valerie Mulcahy scored the game's only goal as the champions opened up a comfortable lead of 1-12 to 0-5.

Sharon Duncan, Armagh, determined to get past Marie O'Connell, Galway. Galway v Armagh, Ladies All Ireland Football Semi Final, Dr Hyde Park, Co. Roscommon. 9 September 2006

Nollaig Cleary and dual star Mary O'Connor were among the point scorers. Laois did get the last four points of the game, but by then Cork had taken their foot off the pedal, content they were heading back to Croke Park on All Ireland Final day thanks to a 1-12 to 0-8 scoreline.

The real story of the semi finals emerged from Dr Hyde Park, Roscommon and not just in the fact that Armagh had beaten hot favourites Galway, but the controversy at the conclusion of a gripping game.

Galway started brightly and opened up an early lead, as the youthful Armagh side seemed overawed by the fact that they were actually in an All Ireland Semi Final. To their credit they gradually got to the pitch of proceedings, mainly through the efforts of the O'Donnell twins, Bronagh and Alma.

The Ulster champions actually hit the front with three points and were further boosted when Maire O'Donnell hit a well-taken goal.

Galway though are an experienced side and responded with a cracking goal from Lisa Coohill and with Gillian Joyce adding points from both play and frees, it was the Tribeswomen who led 1-8 to 1-6 at half-time.

Armagh drew level within four minutes of the resumption and it set the trend for the remainder of the half as the sides traded points in a cracking contest. With time running out Gillian Joyce and Aileen Matthews exchanged points – sides level with the clock inching its way towards the sixty minute mark.

A blow for Armagh when they had Matthews sin-binned with five minutes remaining – advantage Galway. However this absorbing contest had a twist or two left in it yet.

With the sands of time running out Galway attacked, and the ever reliable Barbara Hannon struck what looked like the

winning point. Her immediate reaction was one of glee.

But to the amazement of most people in the ground, the umpire on the near post waved wide, while the other official appeared to signal a point. The referee went with the umpire closest to the shot and did not allow the score. It got worse for Galway.

In one final attack Armagh won a free. The hooter sounded, but as per the rules there was time to take the free.

Up stepped Sharon Duncan and displaying nerves of steel she coolly slotted the ball between the posts, for a dramatic victory for the Ulster champions, 1-13 to 1-12.

Galway were shell shocked. Television and other pictures clearly showed that

Hannon's shot was inside the post and was a point. Their team manager PJ Fahy, vowed to pursue the matter. 'It was definitely a point and we will be lodging an immediate appeal and feel we are entitled to a replay. It's hard to train all year and then be denied in such circumstances.'

Galway's appeal was heard by the Central Council of the Ladies Football Association on the Thursday after the game (Sept 14th) but it was in vain. The Council ruled against the appeal on the basis that there is no provision in the rules to alter the score of a game. So the result stands and it's Armagh v Cork in the final.

Fahy was furious at the decision and slammed the Central Council. 'Once again they have buried their heads in the sand and all we asked for was fair play. If they could have only seen the tears in 17 year-old Barbara Hannon's face after the match, she was inconsolable.'

Historic Final pairing

The TG4 Final will be historic in many ways, not least the pairing.

Cork the champions appearing in their second successive final and on an amazing 25-game unbeaten run in that period – against unfancied Armagh.

Armagh are the reigning All Ireland Junior champions so for the first time ever the Junior and Senior champions will meet in a final.

More history as Cork are bidding for a double double having won the league and championship in 2005 and now are one game away from repeating that feat in 2006.

Five Cork players also stand on the brink of history, having won camogie medals on the second Sunday in September. Briege Corkery, Mary O'Connor, Rena Buckley, Catriona Foley and Angela Walsh, will hope to make it a month to remember by adding a football medal to their collection. Who said the age of the dual player was dead?

What of Armagh? It's been a

Mary O'Connor, Cork, tries to recover the ball despite the attention of Kay O'Reilly, Laois. Cork v Laois, Ladies All Ireland Football Semi Final, O'Connor Park, Tullamore, Co. Offaly. 2 September 2006

Sharon Duncan, Armagh celebrates with team-mates Alma O'Donnell, (8) and Caroline O'Hanlon, (9) after kicking the winning point. Galway v Armagh, Ladies All Ireland Football Semi Final, Dr Hyde Park, Co. Roscommon. 9 September 2006

fairytale rise to the final and one the Orchard County girls will savour and make no mistake – this is a good team who are here to stay.

Ulster men may have drawn a blank in the championship of 2006, but the ladies from Armagh have shown there is still life in the Province.

Junior's big day

In keeping with tradition, the Junior final will act as curtain-raiser to the big game and it's a special day for the ladies from Sligo and Leitrim in the all-Connacht decider. In fact it's a repeat of the Connacht final which was won by Leitrim.

In the respective semi finals, Leitrim beat Longford, while Sligo saw off the challenge of Clare.

Sligo will be hoping it's a case of fourth time lucky as heartbreakingly, they have lost the last three All Ireland finals.

The Final

Played before 25,665 fans, Cork and Armagh produced a tense and exciting final as they battled to win the Brendan Martin Cup.

The Ulster champions, who

were Junior All Ireland champions in 2005, made an excellent start and their powerful play saw them open up an early lead.

Cork got the first score – a Nollaig Cleary point – but struggled for long periods as Armagh tightened their grip on the game. The sides were level on 11 minutes before Armagh struck for the game's opening goal, putting them six points ahead.

However, there was a gradual improvement in Cork's play, helped by a crucial point from Mary O'Connor, and good energetic displays from Briege Corkery and Rena Buckley. By the half-time break, Cork were back in the game as they trailed by only 4 points, Armagh 1-4 Cork 0-3.

Cork maintained their improvement in the second half and it was now Armagh's turn to struggle. Juliet Murphy and Caoimhe Creedon had points for Cork and the comeback was complete when Cleary (later named player of the match) goaled at the second attempt in the 43rd minute.

It was an important score as it gave Cork the lead, plus it coincided with the sin-binning (harshly it must be said) of Armagh's Caoimhe Marley.

To their credit, Armagh drew level when Caroline O'Hanlon kicked a point, but Cork were now playing with more self-assurance and they went two points ahead with eight minutes remaining, thanks to scores from Amanda Murphy and Geraldine O'Flynn.

Armagh battled away. Tennyson pointed to cut the gap to 1, but a couple of timely interventions by splendid Cork captain Juliet Murphy denied them the opportunity to draw level. The champions hung on for a narrow but deserved win.

Cork were winners by 1-7 to 1-6 over gallant Armagh. A special day also for a quartet of Cork players who add Ladies' Football medals to the Senior Camogie medals won on the same pitch a few weeks earlier. An afternoon that Rena Buckley, Briege Corkery, Mary O'Connor and Angela Walsh will cherish.

In fairness to Armagh, they made a supreme effort and were unfortunate to have a player sin-binned at a vital time in the contest. They were also denied what appeared to be a legitimate free late in the game. However,

the Cork players can be proud of their win – coming on a weekend when Cork also won the All Ireland Senior 'B' Camogie title. Double celebrations for the Leeside Ladies.

Final	
Cork	1-7
Armagh	1-6

An historic day also for the ladies from Sligo, who at the third attempt captured the All Ireland Junior title with a win over Connacht rivals Leitrim, who led at half-time by 0-4 to 0-3.

Sligo rejigged their team for the second half and it worked. Leitrim scored only once in the second half, while points from Helena Haran, Therese Marren and Stephanie O'Reilly eased Sligo to a 0-8 to 0-4 win, banishing the memory of the previous two defeats. The ladies from Yeats' County celebrated a famous win.

Look out for Great GAA Moments 2007

- Will the **Kingdom** retain the title in 2007?
- Can **Mayo** conquer Connacht and challenge for the ultimate prize?
- Will **Dublin** emerge from Leinster and challenge for the 2007 title?
- Can **Cork** get revenge on **Kilkenny** or will **Tipperary**, **Galway**, **Clare** or **Limerick** have a say in the outcome?
- Which managers will fall by the wayside, willingly or unwillingly?
- Will **Tyrone** or **Armagh** make a triumphant return?
- Who will be the stars of the leagues and championships of 2007?
- How will the opening up of Croke Park to soccer and rugby in 2007 go down with the GAA and its followers?